PRAYING THROUGH PROVERBS

Wisdom for Men

Rob Thorpe

Praying Through Proverbs - Wisdom for Men
by Rob Thorpe

Published by All In Ministries, Inc.
1 Piedmont Lane
Little Rock, AR 72223

© All In Ministries, Inc. 2025

All rights reserved. No part of this book may be reproduced or transmitted any form or by any means, electronic or mechanical, including photocopying and recording, or by any information storage and retrieval system, without permission in writing from the publisher.

ISBN | 978-1-7359604-5-6

Printed in the United States of America

Bible references quoted from New International Version

Need some wisdom today?

Read the chapter of Proverbs that corresponds to the current day of the month. Afterward, read (pray) the corresponding prayer (outloud is preferable) taking time to think about/ and personalize what you are reading.

What is God speaking to <u>you</u> in this chapter? Write down your thoughts. Remember God promises that if we will Ask, He will give us; if we Seek, we will find, and if we Knock, He will open a door for us (Matthew 7:7-8)

Don't be in a hurry to read through the chapter just to say you did it ... This book is an invitation for you to actually hear God's voice. He loves you and is eager to share His wisdom, and His direction with you ... if you will take the time to listen.

You need wisdom today, right?
How about understanding? Encouragement?
Are you seeking direction about anything going on in your life, in your marriage, job, and family?

Of course you are.

I'm thinking the God Who created the heavens and the earth, Who holds everything together, Who has all wisdom, discernment and understanding - just might have a word for you today (and every day) as his beloved son.

Doesn't it make sense to take a few minutes, sit down with Him, and listen?

PROVERBS 1

1 The proverbs of Solomon son of David, king of Israel:
2 for gaining wisdom and instruction; for understanding words of insight;

3 for receiving instruction in prudent behavior, doing what is right and just and fair;

4 for giving prudence to those who are simple, knowledge and discretion to the young–

5 let the wise listen and add to their learning, and let the discerning get guidance

6 for understanding proverbs and parables, the sayings and riddles of the wise.

7 The fear of the LORD is the beginning of knowledge, but fools despise wisdom and instruction.

8 Listen, my son, to your father's instruction and do not forsake your mother's teaching.

9 They are a garland to grace your head and a chain to adorn your neck.

10 My son, if sinful men entice you, do not give in to them.

11 If they say, "Come along with us; let's lie in wait for innocent blood, let's ambush some harmless soul;

12 let's swallow them alive, like the grave, and whole, like those who go down to the pit;

13 we will get all sorts of valuable things and fill our houses with plunder;

14 cast lots with us; we will all share the loot"–

15 my son, do not go along with them, do not set foot on their paths;

16 for their feet rush into evil, they are swift to shed blood.

17 How useless to spread a net where every bird can see it!

18 These men lie in wait for their own blood; they ambush only themselves!

19 Such are the paths of all who go after ill-gotten gain; it takes away the life of those who get it.

20 Out in the open wisdom calls aloud, she raises her voice in the public square;

21 on top of the wall she cries out, at the city gate she makes her speech:

22 "How long will you who are simple love your simple ways? How long will mockers delight in mockery and fools hate knowledge?

23 Repent at my rebuke! Then I will pour out my thoughts to you, I will make known to you my teachings.

24 But since you refuse to listen when I call and no one pays attention when I stretch out my hand,

25 since you disregard all my advice and do not accept my rebuke,

26 I in turn will laugh when disaster strikes you; I will mock when calamity overtakes you–

27 when calamity overtakes you like a storm, when disaster sweeps over you like a whirlwind, when distress and trouble overwhelm you.

28 "Then they will call to me but I will not answer; they will look for me but will not find me,

29 since they hated knowledge and did not choose to fear the LORD .

30 Since they would not accept my advice and spurned my rebuke,

31 they will eat the fruit of their ways and be filled with the fruit of their schemes.

32 For the waywardness of the simple will kill them, and the complacency of fools will destroy them;

33 but whoever listens to me will live in safety and be at ease, without fear of harm."

Proverbs 1 - Prayer

Father, I come to You today not just to talk–but to listen. I need wisdom Lord, not just any wisdom, not man's wisdom - but Your wisdom. I don't want to go through life making decisions based on what I think or feel, or what others say. Please grant me Your wisdom, along with moral instruction, that I might live skillfully and righteously.

I am desperate for Your instruction Lord, in order to discern wise counsel and guidance from Your Word, from other Christian brothers and mentors. I thank You for the people You've placed in my life to guide me. Whether it's a parent, a mentor, or a spiritual leader–help me to stay teachable and humble.

Would you help me resist temptation today? Keep me from being enticed to walk down any path with men who are not following you - and to choose my companions and friends carefully. Give me the strength to say no when temptation whispers and to stand firm when peer pressure calls. I want to walk the narrow road, even when it's hard.

I acknowledge that all my resources and financial blessings are from You. Allow me Lord, to do my work as unto You, to avoid taking shortcuts, and to be honest and upright in all my financial dealings.

Father, thank You that You love me enough to correct me, and even discipline me when I forsake You and ignore Your instruction. May I be quick to respond to Your rebuke and correction with humility, knowing You discipline those You love. Keep me from straying from You and keep me close enough to hear Your voice and follow Your footsteps.

I ask that You pour out Your thoughts to me and make Your words known to me today, Lord. May I pay close attention and never neglect Your advice.

I desire to take time to listen today, and to make our relationship my top priority. Please help me to hear and to gladly and quickly obey what You tell me to do.

Thank You Father, that I can live securely, without fear of harm today as I listen to You. Open my ears, Lord, that I may hear You above the constant noise and distraction all around me.

What I'm hearing God say today:

PROVERBS 2

1 My son, if you accept my words and store up my commands within you,

2 turning your ear to wisdom and applying your heart to understanding–

3 indeed, if you call out for insight and cry aloud for understanding,

4 and if you look for it as for silver and search for it as for hidden treasure,

5 then you will understand the fear of the LORD and find the knowledge of God.

6 For the LORD gives wisdom; from his mouth come knowledge and understanding.

7 He holds success in store for the upright, he is a shield to those whose walk is blameless,

8 for he guards the course of the just and protects the way of his faithful ones.

9 Then you will understand what is right and just and fair–every good path.

10 For wisdom will enter your heart, and knowledge will be pleasant to your soul.

11 Discretion will protect you, and understanding will guard you.

12 Wisdom will save you from the ways of wicked men, from men whose words are perverse,

13 who have left the straight paths to walk in dark ways,

14 who delight in doing wrong and rejoice in the perverseness of evil,

15 whose paths are crooked and who are devious in their ways.

16 Wisdom will save you also from the adulterous woman, from the wayward woman with her seductive words,

17 who has left the partner of her youth and ignored the covenant she made before God.

18 Surely her house leads down to death and her paths to the spirits of the dead.

19 None who go to her return or attain the paths of life.

20 Thus you will walk in the ways of the good and keep to the paths of the righteous.

21 For the upright will live in the land, and the blameless will remain in it;

22 but the wicked will be cut off from the land, and the unfaithful will be torn from it.

Proverbs 2 - Prayer

Father God, thank You for being the source of all wisdom. Today, I come to You as a man seeking more than head knowledge–I want the kind of understanding that transforms how I live. Your Word tells me that if I accept Your words and store up Your commands in my heart, if I tune my ear to wisdom and apply my heart to understanding, I will find the treasure that is only found in fearing You.

Lord, I'm asking–help me seek Your truth more passionately than I chase success, security, or approval. I know You give wisdom, and from Your mouth come knowledge and understanding. You are my shield when I walk in integrity, and You guard my steps when I live with purpose.

Teach me to delight in doing what is right. Give me discernment to recognize the paths that lead to life and those that end in regret. Protect me from the seductive voices that pull me away from You–the lies of this world, the shortcuts of sin, and the easy road that leads to destruction.

God, I want to be a man who walks in righteousness, who loves truth, who stands firm even when the crowd moves the other way. Help me walk the path of the just, and let Your wisdom enter my heart so that discretion will protect me and understanding will guard me.

Surround me with Your truth. Lead me away from compromise, and strengthen my resolve to live a life that honors You. I want to be a man who finishes strong–faithful, wise, and rooted in Your Word.

Thank You that Your ways are always good, and Your promises never fail. I trust You to lead me, shape me, and use me for Your purpose today.

What I'm hearing God say today:

PROVERBS 3

1 My son, do not forget my teaching, but keep my commands in your heart,

2 for they will prolong your life many years and bring you peace and prosperity.

3 Let love and faithfulness never leave you; bind them around your neck, write them on the tablet of your heart.

4 Then you will win favor and a good name in the sight of God and man.

5 Trust in the LORD with all your heart and lean not on your own understanding;

6 in all your ways submit to him, and he will make your paths straight.

7 Do not be wise in your own eyes; fear the LORD and shun evil.

8 This will bring health to your body and nourishment to your bones.

9 Honor the LORD with your wealth, with the first fruits of all your crops;

10 then your barns will be filled to overflowing, and your vats will brim over with new wine.

11 My son, do not despise the LORD's discipline, and do not resent his rebuke,

12 because the LORD disciplines those he loves, as a father the son he delights in.

13 Blessed are those who find wisdom, those who gain understanding,

14 for she is more profitable than silver and yields better returns than gold.

15 She is more precious than rubies; nothing you desire can compare with her.

16 Long life is in her right hand; in her left hand are riches and honor.

17 Her ways are pleasant ways, and all her paths are peace.

18 She is a tree of life to those who take hold of her; those who hold her fast will be blessed.

19 By wisdom the LORD laid the earth's foundations, by understanding he set the heavens in place;

20 by his knowledge the watery depths were divided, and the clouds let drop the dew.

21 My son, do not let wisdom and understanding out of your sight, preserve sound judgment and discretion;

22 they will be life for you, an ornament to grace your neck.

23 Then you will go on your way in safety, and your foot will not stumble.

24 When you lie down, you will not be afraid; when you lie down, your sleep will be sweet.

25 Have no fear of sudden disaster or of the ruin that overtakes the wicked,

26 for the LORD will be at your side and will keep your foot from being snared.

27 Do not withhold good from those to whom it is due, when it is in your power to act.

28 Do not say to your neighbor, "Come back tomorrow and I'll give it to you"– when you already have it with you.

29 Do not plot harm against your neighbor, who lives trustfully near you.

30 Do not accuse anyone for no reason— when they have done you no harm.

31 Do not envy the violent or choose any of their ways.

32 For the LORD detests the perverse but takes the upright into his confidence.

33 The LORD's curse is on the house of the wicked, but he blesses the home of the righteous.

34 He mocks proud mockers but shows favor to the humble and oppressed.

35 The wise inherit honor, but fools get only shame.

Proverbs 3 - Prayer

Father, help me today to remember Your teaching and empower me to keep Your commandments. Allow me to walk in mercy and truth throughout this day, that I might receive Your blessing and favor.

I completely trust You, Lord, and desire not to lean on my own understanding. Help me to recognize Your presence and Your leadership today, and to make You known in all my interactions with others. I am desperate to walk in Your wisdom and not my own.

I walk in awe and reverence of You Lord, and ask you today to give me the strength to turn away from evil and the temptations and distractions Satan puts in my way.

Father, all that I have is from You. My job, my income, my financial security - all my resources are a gift from Your hand. In obedience to Your Word, I commit to honor you by giving You the first fruits of all my increase. I desire to be a cheerful giver, and to live generously with the money, time and resources You have blessed me with.

Thank You that as Your son You discipline me when I need it, because You love me and want only the best for me. Keep me close Lord, and keep me from straying from You and going my own way.

Again today Lord, I ask for Your wisdom and divine understanding as I deal with difficult circumstances, difficult people, and the disappointments of life. I am desperate for Your sound wisdom and discretion. You are the sole source of my security, peace and joy.

As I walk with You and draw upon Your wisdom, You assure me that I will not stumble, nor walk in fear - even my sleep will be pleasant. I do not have to be anxious or fearful concerning the future - because You are sovereign and rule over all that is ahead for me. You are the source of my confidence and hope.

Open my eyes for opportunities to be generous to others and to walk in humility before You. I trust You with this day, Lord. Guide my thoughts, strengthen my hands, and fill my heart with peace. I choose to acknowledge You in all I do–and I believe You'll take care of the rest.

What I'm hearing God say today:

PROVERBS 4

1 Listen, my sons, to a father's instruction; pay attention and gain understanding.

2 I give you sound learning, so do not forsake my teaching.

3 For I too was a son to my father, still tender, and cherished by my mother.

4 Then he taught me, and he said to me, "Take hold of my words with all your heart; keep my commands, and you will live.

5 Get wisdom, get understanding; do not forget my words or turn away from them.

6 Do not forsake wisdom, and she will protect you; love her, and she will watch over you.

7 The beginning of wisdom is this: Get wisdom. Though it cost all you have, get understanding.

8 Cherish her, and she will exalt you; embrace her, and she will honor you.

9 She will give you a garland to grace your head and present you with a glorious crown."

10 Listen, my son, accept what I say, and the years of your life will be many.

11 I instruct you in the way of wisdom and lead you along straight paths.

12 When you walk, your steps will not be hampered; when you run, you will not stumble.

13 Hold on to instruction, do not let it go; guard it well, for it is your life.

14 Do not set foot on the path of the wicked or walk in the way of evildoers.

15 Avoid it, do not travel on it; turn from it and go on your way.

16 For they cannot rest until they do evil; they are robbed of sleep till they make someone stumble.

17 They eat the bread of wickedness and drink the wine of violence.

18 The path of the righteous is like the morning sun, shining ever brighter till the full light of day.

19 But the way of the wicked is like deep darkness; they do not know what makes them stumble.

20 My son, pay attention to what I say; turn your ear to my words.

21 Do not let them out of your sight, keep them within your heart;

22f or they are life to those who find them and health to one's whole body.

23 Above all else, guard your heart, for everything you do flows from it.

24 Keep your mouth free of perversity; keep corrupt talk far from your lips.

25 Let your eyes look straight ahead; fix your gaze directly before you.

26 Give careful thought to the paths for your feet and be steadfast in all your ways.

27 Do not turn to the right or the left; keep your foot from evil.

Proverbs 4 - Prayer

Father, give me ears to hear Your wise instruction and gain discernment from Your Word, and from other righteous men in my life.

More importantly Lord, grant me the strength and grace to keep the commands You speak to me, so that I might live with wisdom and understanding. Only then will I have the strength and courage to walk a straight path with You through this evil landscape of life.

Thank You that Your words protect me and guard me. Help me make time in Your word a top priority today. I am desperate for Your guidance and wisdom. Your words alone are life and healing, and my heart's desire is to live according to them.

Help me Father, to avoid the way of the wicked and not be attracted in the least by anything in their lives.

Empower me today to guard my heart above all things, to consider my thoughts and take them captive to the obedience of Christ. I know that what resides in my heart eventually comes out of me. So purify my thoughts. Let my mouth speak words of truth and life, and guard my lips from speaking lies or hurtful words.

Keep my eyes focused on You, Lord, and grant me the courage to completely trust Your leadership and sovereign plan for my life.

Father, I thank You for Your wisdom, which leads me, protects me, and matures me. Help me to not only hear it–but to live it.

I trust that as I follow You, the path ahead will grow brighter, and I will become more like the man You created me to be.

What I'm hearing God say today:

PROVERBS 5

1 My son, pay attention to my wisdom, turn your ear to my words of insight,

2 that you may maintain discretion and your lips may preserve knowledge.

3 For the lips of the adulterous woman drip honey, and her speech is smoother than oil;

4 but in the end she is bitter as gall, sharp as a double-edged sword.

5 Her feet go down to death; her steps lead straight to the grave.

6 She gives no thought to the way of life; her paths wander aimlessly, but she does not know it.

7 Now then, my sons, listen to me; do not turn aside from what I say.

8 Keep to a path far from her, do not go near the door of her house,

9 lest you lose your honor to others and your years to one who is cruel,

10 lest strangers feast on your wealth and your toil enrich the house of another.

11 At the end of your life you will groan, when your flesh and body are spent.

12 You will say, "How I hated discipline! How my heart spurned correction!

13 I would not obey my teachers or turn my ear to my instructors.

14 And I was soon in serious trouble in the assembly of God's people."

15 Drink water from your own cistern, running water from your own well.

16 Should your springs overflow in the streets, your streams of water in the public squares?

17 Let them be yours alone, never to be shared with strangers.

18 May your fountain be blessed, and may you rejoice in the wife of your youth.

19 A loving doe, a graceful deer— may her breasts satisfy you always, may you ever be intoxicated with her love.

20 Why, my son, be intoxicated with another man's wife? Why embrace the bosom of a wayward woman?

21 For your ways are in full view of the LORD, and he examines all your paths.

22 The evil deeds of the wicked ensnare them; the cords of their sins hold them fast.

23 For lack of discipline they will die, led astray by their own great folly.

Proverbs 5 - Prayer

Father, help me be attentive to Your wisdom today and to pay close attention to Your divine understanding. I still myself in Your presence and ask that You speak to me now.

Keep me from the allure and rationalization of moral sin today. Seductive and adulterous images surround me and call out to me for attention, and I need Your strength to remain a man of moral character and integrity. I want to live with integrity, not just in public but in private–especially when it comes to purity, faithfulness, and the desires of my heart.

Shout to me, Lord when I am tempted to look upon women or images of women that the enemy uses to divert my affection and distract my mind from focusing on my walk with You, and my commitment to my wife. God, guard my eyes, my thoughts, and my steps. Don't let me wander near temptation. Help me build boundaries that protect my soul and honor You.

I rejoice today in my wife and praise You for bringing my perfect helper to complete me and help shape me more into Your image. She is Your daughter, and I humbly ask that You empower me to love her as Christ loves His church, and to lay my life down for her today. Show me how to best do that, and how to be the husband she deserves.

You created marriage Father, and I know it is Your divine workshop for making me into the man You created me to be - a man who resembles Jesus more today than yesterday.

I also know that Satan hates marriage because it represents the love Jesus has for his bride, and he is working day and night to destroy my marriage, my family, my witness, and my legacy.

I ask for Your divine protection over my marriage relationship Father, and know that You provide everything I need to enjoy the marriage You intend me to have, and be able to bring You glory by it. Help me to be alert to the devil's schemes today, and empower me by Your Spirit to walk in integrity.

My ways are in full view of You. May my thoughts, my words, and my actions be pleasing to You, and bring You glory today.

What I'm hearing God say today:

PROVERBS 6

1 My son, if you have put up security for your neighbor, if you have shaken hands in pledge for a stranger,

2 you have been trapped by what you said, ensnared by the words of your mouth.

3 So do this, my son, to free yourself, since you have fallen into your neighbor's hands: Go–to the point of exhaustion– and give your neighbor no rest!

4 Allow no sleep to your eyes, no slumber to your eyelids.

5 Free yourself, like a gazelle from the hand of the hunter, like a bird from the snare of the fowler.

6 Go to the ant, you sluggard; consider its ways and be wise!

7 It has no commander, no overseer or ruler,

8 yet it stores its provisions in summer and gathers its food at harvest.

9 How long will you lie there, you sluggard? When will you get up from your sleep?

10 A little sleep, a little slumber, a little folding of the hands to rest–

11 and poverty will come on you like a thief and scarcity like an armed man.

12 A troublemaker and a villain, who goes about with a corrupt mouth,

13 who winks maliciously with his eye, signals with his feet and motions with his fingers,

14 who plots evil with deceit in his heart— he always stirs up conflict.

15 Therefore disaster will overtake him in an instant; he will suddenly be destroyed–without remedy.

16 There are six things the LORD hates, seven that are detestable to him:

17 haughty eyes, a lying tongue, hands that shed innocent blood,

18 a heart that devises wicked schemes, feet that are quick to rush into evil,

19 a false witness who pours out lies and a person who stirs up conflict in the community.

20 My son, keep your father's command and do not forsake your mother's teaching.

21 Bind them always on your heart; fasten them around your neck.

22 When you walk, they will guide you; when you sleep, they will watch over you; when you awake, they will speak to you.

23 For this command is a lamp, this teaching is a light, and correction and instruction are the way to life,

24 keeping you from your neighbor's wife, from the smooth talk of a wayward woman.

25 Do not lust in your heart after her beauty or let her captivate you with her eyes.

26 For a prostitute can be had for a loaf of bread, but another man's wife preys on your very life.

27 Can a man scoop fire into his lap without his clothes being burned?

28 Can a man walk on hot coals without his feet being scorched?

29 So is he who sleeps with another man's wife; no one who touches her will go unpunished.

30 People do not despise a thief if he steals to satisfy his hunger when he is starving.

31 Yet if he is caught, he must pay sevenfold, though it costs him all the wealth of his house.

32 But a man who commits adultery has no sense; whoever does so destroys himself.

33 Blows and disgrace are his lot, and his shame will never be wiped away.

34 For jealousy arouses a husband's fury, and he will show no mercy when he takes revenge.

35 He will not accept any compensation; he will refuse a bribe, however great it is.

Proverbs 6 - Prayer

Father, I acknowledge that everything I have comes from You. I look to You for wisdom today to help me steward my finances well. Help me to listen for Your voice, and heed Your instruction regarding my money and finances.

Help me to work diligently as unto You today, and allow me to bring You honor as I deal with customers, colleagues and those in authority over me. Help me not be lazy or distracted, wasting time or making excuses. Instead, give me a heart that plans ahead, works diligently, and honors You in every task, no matter how small.

Keep me from evil people and those who would entice me to turn from You. May I not be attracted to anything in their lives. I desire only what You have for me today and trust Your sovereign plan for my future.

May my heart remain humble and my lips speak the truth in all my interactions with others today. Help me to live in peace with the people in my life and walk according to Your Word. Help me hear Your voice as You lead me today. Watch over me and guide me in all my ways.

Lord, I need You every hour. I need Your Word to guide me, Your Spirit to strengthen me, and Your grace to forgive me when I fall. Help me remember: the path of wisdom is not just smart–it's godly. And godliness always leads to peace, purpose, and protection.

Lord, temptation is all around me. The world shouts its voice and tells me to come and join in. The adulterous woman lives in my phone. I carry her with me wherever I go. Help me today to remove any and every opportunity available for me to see her and be lured into her chambers. When temptation comes–especially sexual temptation–remind me of what's at stake. Give me the courage to run and not flirt with danger.

Strengthen my heart, guard my thoughts, and grant that I will remain faithful to You - and to the marriage covenant I vowed to You and to my wife and family.

What I'm hearing God say today:

PROVERBS 7

1 My son, keep my words and store up my commands within you.

2 Keep my commands and you will live; guard my teachings as the apple of your eye.

3 Bind them on your fingers; write them on the tablet of your heart.

4 Say to wisdom, "You are my sister," and to insight, "You are my relative."

5 They will keep you from the adulterous woman, from the wayward woman with her seductive words.

6 At the window of my house I looked down through the lattice.

7 I saw among the simple, I noticed among the young men, a youth who had no sense.

8 He was going down the street near her corner, walking along in the direction of her house

9 at twilight, as the day was fading, as the dark of night set in.

10 Then out came a woman to meet him, dressed like a prostitute and with crafty intent.

11 (She is unruly and defiant, her feet never stay at home;

12 now in the street, now in the squares, at every corner she lurks.)

13 She took hold of him and kissed him and with a brazen face she said:

14 "Today I fulfilled my vows, and I have food from my fellowship offering at home.

15 So I came out to meet you; I looked for you and have found you!

16 I have covered my bed with colored linens from Egypt.

17 I have perfumed my bed with myrrh, aloes and cinnamon.

18 Come, let's drink deeply of love till morning; let's enjoy ourselves with love!

19 My husband is not at home; he has gone on a long journey.

20 He took his purse filled with money and will not be home till full moon."

21 With persuasive words she led him astray; she seduced him with her smooth talk.

22 All at once he followed her like an ox going to the slaughter, like a deer [a] stepping into a noose [b]

23 till an arrow pierces his liver, like a bird darting into a snare, little knowing it will cost him his life.

24 Now then, my sons, listen to me; pay attention to what I say.

25 Do not let your heart turn to her ways or stray into her paths.

26 Many are the victims she has brought down; her slain are a mighty throng.

27 Her house is a highway to the grave, leading down to the chambers of death.

Proverbs 7 - Prayer

Father, would You renew my devotion and passion for Your Word today? Help me not be content to simply read it, but to linger in its truth and store it up in my heart. Without Your strength, Lord, I am powerless to keep Your commands and obey Your instructions.

I am desperate for Your wisdom and divine understanding - to guide me and keep me on the right and righteous path today. May I never become enticed by the attention or affection of someone other than my wife, or flirt with such destructive thoughts and lies from the enemy.

Lord, like the young man in this Proverb, it's easy to walk near danger and tell myself I'm strong enough to handle it. But I'm not. You know my heart. You know how easily I can be drawn in by what looks good but leads to destruction.

Keep my feet far from paths that lead to sin. Remind me that not everything that looks appealing is from You. Help me recognize the seduction of shortcuts, of secret sins, of voices that flatter but deceive. Give me the discernment to see through the lies and the courage to walk away–even when no one else sees.

Apart from Your Word I quickly become a fool and open myself up to temptation and every evil path. Keep my heart in Your Word, Lord, and give me the strength to keep my way pure today.

Father, grant me Your strength today to guard my heart, my thoughts and my affections. I bring them all under Your authority and ask that You empower me to resist the enemy and walk in the authority You have granted me as Your son.

...but each man is tempted, when he is drawn away by his own lust, and enticed. Then the lust, when it hath conceived, bears sin: and the sin, when it is full grown, brings forth death. James 1:14-15

What I'm hearing God say today:

PROVERBS 8

1 Does not wisdom call out? Does not understanding raise her voice?

2 At the highest point along the way, where the paths meet, she takes her stand;

3 beside the gate leading into the city, at the entrance, she cries aloud:

4 "To you, O people, I call out; I raise my voice to all mankind.

5 You who are simple, gain prudence; you who are foolish, set your hearts on it.

6 Listen, for I have trustworthy things to say; I open my lips to speak what is right.

7 My mouth speaks what is true, for my lips detest wickedness.

8 All the words of my mouth are just; none of them is crooked or perverse.

9 To the discerning all of them are right; they are upright to those who have found knowledge.

10 Choose my instruction instead of silver, knowledge rather than choice gold,

11 for wisdom is more precious than rubies, and nothing you desire can compare with her.

12 "I, wisdom, dwell together with prudence; I possess knowledge and discretion.

13 To fear the LORD is to hate evil; I hate pride and arrogance, evil behavior and perverse speech.

14 Counsel and sound judgment are mine; I have insight, I have power.

15 By me kings reign and rulers issue decrees that are just;

16 by me princes govern, and nobles—all who rule on earth.

17 I love those who love me, and those who seek me find me.

18 With me are riches and honor, enduring wealth and prosperity.

19 My fruit is better than fine gold; what I yield surpasses choice silver.

20 I walk in the way of righteousness, along the paths of justice,

21 bestowing a rich inheritance on those who love me and making their treasuries full.

22 "The LORD brought me forth as the first of his works, before his deeds of old;

23 I was formed long ages ago, at the very beginning, when the world came to be.

24 When there were no watery depths, I was given birth, when there were no springs overflowing with water;

25 before the mountains were settled in place, before the hills, I was given birth,

26 before he made the world or its fields or any of the dust of the earth.

27 I was there when he set the heavens in place, when he marked out the horizon on the face of the deep,

28 when he established the clouds above and fixed securely the fountains of the deep,

29 when he gave the sea its boundary so the waters would not overstep his command, and when he marked out the foundations of the earth.

30 Then I was constantly at his side. I was filled with delight day after day, rejoicing always in his presence,

31 rejoicing in his whole world and delighting in mankind.

32 "Now then, my children, listen to me; blessed are those who keep my ways.

33 Listen to my instruction and be wise; do not disregard it.

34 Blessed are those who listen to me, watching daily at my doors, waiting at my doorway.

35 For those who find me find life and receive favor from the LORD.

36 But those who fail to find me harm themselves; all who hate me love death.

Proverbs 8 - Prayer

Father of all wisdom, I call out to You today and ask that You allow me to hear Your voice of wisdom and understanding. You alone speak excellent things and utter what is right and true.

I desperately need Your discernment and direction regarding the many issues and decisions facing me. I quiet my heart now Father, and desire to receive Your instruction, knowledge and wisdom.

Teach me to hate evil and reject every semblance of pride that tempts me today. Allow me to walk in Your sound wisdom and counsel - not being wise in my own eyes.

Thank You for Your sovereign reign over all things and over my life.

I seek You diligently today Lord, and know that You will provide everything I need to live righteously and bear fruit for Your kingdom. Thank You for Your promised blessings as I seek You and learn to walk in Your ways.

Allow me to shut out the noise and busyness that crowd my thoughts and try to drowned out my time with You. Help me to listen closely for Your voice, and never neglect time in Your presence. I watch for You every day, Father, and eagerly wait to receive everything You desire to speak to me.

Thank You that You promise to never leave or forsake me; to lead me along paths of righteousness, and to allow me to find You if I seek You.

Thank You for filling me with Your Spirit, for adopting me as Your son, and granting me the privilege of being a joint heir with Your Son, Jesus.

I am forever grateful that You chose me, sent Your Son to pay the penalty for my sin, and allow me to be seated with Him, in heavenly places, at Your right hand. I am honored to be Your son, and pray today that my life may bring You honor.

What I'm hearing God say today:

PROVERBS 9

1 Wisdom has built her house; she has set up its seven pillars.

2 She has prepared her meat and mixed her wine; she has also set her table.

3 She has sent out her servants, and she calls from the highest point of the city,

4 "Let all who are simple come to my house!" To those who have no sense she says,

5 "Come, eat my food and drink the wine I have mixed.

6 Leave your simple ways and you will live; walk in the way of insight."

7 Whoever corrects a mocker invites insults; whoever rebukes the wicked incurs abuse.

8 Do not rebuke mockers or they will hate you; rebuke the wise and they will love you.

9 Instruct the wise and they will be wiser still; teach the righteous and they will add to their learning.

10 The fear of the LORD is the beginning of wisdom, and knowledge of the Holy One is understanding.

11 For through wisdom your days will be many, and years will be added to your life.

12 If you are wise, your wisdom will reward you; if you are a mocker, you alone will suffer.

13 Folly is an unruly woman; she is simple and knows nothing.

14 She sits at the door of her house, on a seat at the highest point of the city,

15 calling out to those who pass by, who go straight on their way,

16 "Let all who are simple come to my house!" To those who have no sense she says,

17 "Stolen water is sweet; food eaten in secret is delicious!"

18 But little do they know that the dead are there, that her guests are deep in the realm of the dead.

Proverbs 9 - Prayer

Father, allow me to walk in Your wisdom again today. Help me to abandon all my selfish, foolish ways and to walk in the way of understanding. In all my interactions and decisions, allow me to hear Your voice and to follow Your words of discernment and protection.

Grant that I may walk in reverence and holy fear before You. and refrain from folly and from foolish choices of any kind. I acknowledge that real understanding starts when I humble myself before You.

You promise to add years to my life as I walk in Your wisdom. Motivate me even more Lord to stay close to You, listen to Your voice, and obey what You tell me. So Father, make me teachable. When I'm challenged, let me listen–not get defensive. When I'm wrong, help me admit it and learn from it. Because a wise man listens, and by doing so, becomes even wiser.

Father, my culture is full of folly. It calls to me daily to take an easy path, to avoid difficulty and to compromise in order to enjoy life. Folly shouts from social media, from the entertainment industry, from business and government. Help me hear wisdom's voice over all the noise of this world. Give me the courage to turn toward the path that leads to life.

Folly's message calls for abandoning my faith and avoiding the hard work of obedience to You. It is obvious that her message is straight from the lying, deceiving mouth of Satan, and his relentless assault on my faith.

Give me strength today, Father, to shut my ears to her message of death and turn my heart and mind even more resolutely toward my pursuit of an abundant life with You.

But mark this: There will be terrible times in the last days. People will be lovers of themselves, lovers of money, boastful, proud, abusive, disobedient to their parents, ungrateful, unholy, without love, unforgiving, slanderous, without self-control, brutal, not lovers of the good, treacherous, rash, conceited, lovers of pleasure rather than lovers of God– having a form of godliness but denying its power. Have nothing to do with such people.   2 Timothy 3:1-5

What I'm hearing God say today:

PROVERBS 10

1 The proverbs of Solomon: A wise son brings joy to his father, but a foolish son brings grief to his mother.

2 Ill-gotten treasures have no lasting value, but righteousness delivers from death.

3 The LORD does not let the righteous go hungry, but he thwarts the craving of the wicked.

4 Lazy hands make for poverty, but diligent hands bring wealth.

5 He who gathers crops in summer is a prudent son, but he who sleeps during harvest is a disgraceful son.

6 Blessings crown the head of the righteous, but violence overwhelms the mouth of the wicked.

7 The name of the righteous is used in blessings, but the name of the wicked will rot.

8 The wise in heart accept commands, but a chattering fool comes to ruin.

9 Whoever walks in integrity walks securely, but whoever takes crooked paths will be found out.

10 Whoever winks maliciously causes grief, and a chattering fool comes to ruin.

11 The mouth of the righteous is a fountain of life, but the mouth of the wicked conceals violence.

12 Hatred stirs up conflict, but love covers over all wrongs.

13 Wisdom is found on the lips of the discerning, but a rod is for the back of one who has no sense.

14 The wise store up knowledge, but the mouth of a fool invites ruin.

15 The wealth of the rich is their fortified city, but poverty is the ruin of the poor.

16 The wages of the righteous is life, but the earnings of the wicked are sin and death.

17 Whoever heeds discipline shows the way to life, but whoever ignores correction leads others astray.

18 Whoever conceals hatred with lying lips and spreads slander is a fool.

19 Sin is not ended by multiplying words, but the prudent hold their tongues.

20 The tongue of the righteous is choice silver, but the heart of the wicked is of little value.

21 The lips of the righteous nourish many, but fools die for lack of sense.

22 The blessing of the LORD brings wealth, without painful toil for it.

23 A fool finds pleasure in wicked schemes, but a person of understanding delights in wisdom.

24 What the wicked dread will overtake them; what the righteous desire will be granted.

25 When the storm has swept by, the wicked are gone, but the righteous stand firm forever.

26 As vinegar to the teeth and smoke to the eyes, so are sluggards to those who send them.

27 The fear of the LORD adds length to life, but the years of the wicked are cut short.

28 The prospect of the righteous is joy, but the hopes of the wicked come to nothing.

29 The way of the LORD is a refuge for the blameless, but it is the ruin of those who do evil.

30 The righteous will never be uprooted, but the wicked will not remain in the land.

31 From the mouth of the righteous comes the fruit of wisdom, but a perverse tongue will be silenced.

32 The lips of the righteous know what finds favor, but the mouth of the wicked only what is perverse.

Proverbs 10 - Prayer

Father, Your Word cuts deep–it divides the way of the fool from the way of the wise. God, I want to walk the path of the wise. I want to be the kind of man who lives with purpose, who loves fiercely, who speaks life, and who stands his ground when it counts.

So I ask You–train me. Speak to the deep places in me.

Don't let me chase after empty things–money that disappears, success that fades, applause that dies. Remind me again and again: it's Your blessing that brings real wealth, and it comes without the sorrow of compromise. I don't want counterfeit riches. I want the real thing–Your favor, Your presence, Your smile on my life.

Teach me to work with my hands and my heart. Drive out the laziness, the apathy, the distractions that steal from my calling. Let me be a man who shows up–at home, at work, in the moments that matter.

Make me a man of truth. Let my words carry weight. May I speak life, not death. May I offer blessing, not harm. Keep me from the foolish talk that wounds, the sarcasm that hides fear, and the silence that refuses to engage. Let my mouth be a river of life, flowing from a heart anchored in You.

Father, discipline me when I need it. Correct me when I wander. I want to be the kind of man who welcomes Your correction because I know it's love. I want to grow, not just get by.

Surround me with other men who walk uprightly. And let me be a shelter for others–a man whose presence brings calm, whose life whispers of You even when I don't say a word. This Proverb says the memory of the righteous is a blessing–God, let my story, my presence, my legacy be something that speaks well of You.

And when trouble comes, help me stand. Root me deep. Let me be unshakable–not because I'm strong, but because I'm Yours.

I renounce the way of wickedness, cowardice, and compromise. I choose wisdom. I choose the narrow road. I choose You.

What I'm hearing God say today:

PROVERBS 11

1 The LORD detests dishonest scales, but accurate weights find favor with him.

2 When pride comes, then comes disgrace, but with humility comes wisdom.

3 The integrity of the upright guides them, but the unfaithful are destroyed by their duplicity.

4 Wealth is worthless in the day of wrath, but righteousness delivers from death.

5 The righteousness of the blameless makes their paths straight, but the wicked are brought down by their own wickedness.

6 The righteousness of the upright delivers them, but the unfaithful are trapped by evil desires.

7 Hopes placed in mortals die with them; all the promise of their power comes to nothing.

8 The righteous person is rescued from trouble, and it falls on the wicked instead.

9 With their mouths the godless destroy their neighbors, but through knowledge the righteous escape.

10 When the righteous prosper, the city rejoices; when the wicked perish, there are shouts of joy.

11 Through the blessing of the upright a city is exalted, but by the mouth of the wicked it is destroyed.

12 Whoever derides their neighbor has no sense, but the one who has understanding holds their tongue.

13 A gossip betrays a confidence, but a trustworthy person keeps a secret.

14 For lack of guidance a nation falls, but victory is won through many advisers.

15 Whoever puts up security for a stranger will surely suffer, but whoever refuses to shake hands in pledge is safe.

16 A kindhearted woman gains honor, but ruthless men gain only wealth.

17 Those who are kind benefit themselves, but the cruel bring ruin on themselves.

18 A wicked person earns deceptive wages, but the one who sows righteousness reaps a sure reward.

19 Truly the righteous attain life, but whoever pursues evil finds death.

20 The LORD detests those whose hearts are perverse, but he delights in those whose ways are blameless.

21 Be sure of this: The wicked will not go unpunished, but those who are righteous will go free.

22 Like a gold ring in a pig's snout is a beautiful woman who shows no discretion.

23 The desire of the righteous ends only in good, but the hope of the wicked only in wrath.

24 One person gives freely, yet gains even more; another withholds unduly, but comes to poverty.

25 A generous person will prosper; whoever refreshes others will be refreshed.

26 People curse the one who hoards grain, but they pray God's blessing on the one who is willing to sell.

27 Whoever seeks good finds favor, but evil comes to one who searches for it.

28 Those who trust in their riches will fall, but the righteous will thrive like a green leaf.

29 Whoever brings ruin on their family will inherit only wind, and the fool will be servant to the wise.

30 The fruit of the righteous is a tree of life, and the one who is wise saves lives.

31 If the righteous receive their due on earth, how much more the ungodly and the sinner!

Proverbs 11 - Prayer

Father, once again—I stand before You, a man in the making. A man at war. Not just with the world around me, but with the war within—between who I am and who You're calling me to become. And I hear the call of Proverbs 11 like a trumpet in the fog: Walk uprightly. Live with honor. Choose the narrow way.

God, I don't want to live a life of pretense. I don't want to wear a mask, play the game, or chase after things that glitter but rot from the inside. Your Word says You hate dishonest scales—but You delight in honesty, in truth, in men who live with nothing to hide. I want to be that kind of man—true through and through. Strip away the false. Burn off the fake. What's left, Lord—let it be real. Let it be Yours.

You say integrity guides the upright. Let it guide me today. Let it be my compass when the path is unclear, when no one's watching, when shortcuts whisper. And when pride comes knocking, don't let me answer. I know pride leads to a fall—I've seen it in others, I've tasted it myself. Give me the humility that invites Your wisdom. Make me teachable Father.

Let me walk in righteousness, not for applause, but because it is the way that leads to life. Let me be the kind of man who rescues—not just physically, but spiritually. A man who pulls others out of the quicksand of this world and points them to You.

God, this world is full of noise, deceit, and schemes. I don't want to scheme—I want to serve. I don't want to get ahead—I want to go deeper. Teach me to be generous—not just with money, but with my time, my strength, my heart. You say a generous man prospers, and the one who refreshes others will be refreshed. So, Father, make me a fountain, not a dam. Let my life flow outward, not inward.

Make me a man of quiet confidence—not in myself, but in You. Not loud with opinions, but steady with truth and in action. You say the righteous stand firm even in death—let me be that rooted, that secure, that free.

Father, when I fall, lift me up. When I stray, call me back. Let righteousness be the road I travel, not just an idea I admire. You said the fruit of the righteous is a tree of life—let me be a tree that gives shade, bears fruit, and stands strong in every season.

What I'm hearing God say today:

PROVERBS 12

1 Whoever loves discipline loves knowledge, but whoever hates correction is stupid.

2 Good people obtain favor from the LORD, but he condemns those who devise wicked schemes.

3 No one can be established through wickedness, but the righteous cannot be uprooted.

4 A wife of noble character is her husband's crown, but a disgraceful wife is like decay in his bones.

5 The plans of the righteous are just, but the advice of the wicked is deceitful.

6 The words of the wicked lie in wait for blood, but the speech of the upright rescues them.

7 The wicked are overthrown and are no more, but the house of the righteous stands firm.

8 A person is praised according to their prudence, and one with a warped mind is despised.

9 Better to be a nobody and yet have a servant than pretend to be somebody and have no food.

10 The righteous care for the needs of their animals, but the kindest acts of the wicked are cruel.

11 Those who work their land will have abundant food, but those who chase fantasies have no sense.

12 The wicked desire the stronghold of evildoers, but the root of the righteous endures.

13 Evildoers are trapped by their sinful talk, and so the innocent escape trouble.

14 From the fruit of their lips people are filled with good things, and the work of their hands brings them reward.

15 The way of fools seems right to them, but the wise listen to advice.

16 Fools show their annoyance at once, but the prudent overlook an insult.

17 An honest witness tells the truth, but a false witness tells lies.

18 The words of the reckless pierce like swords, but the tongue of the wise brings healing.

19 Truthful lips endure forever, but a lying tongue lasts only a moment.

20 Deceit is in the hearts of those who plot evil, but those who promote peace have joy.

21 No harm overtakes the righteous, but the wicked have their fill of trouble.

22 The LORD detests lying lips, but he delights in people who are trustworthy.

23 The prudent keep their knowledge to themselves, but a fool's heart blurts out folly.

24 Diligent hands will rule, but laziness ends in forced labor.

25 Anxiety weighs down the heart, but a kind word cheers it up.

26 The righteous choose their friends carefully, but the way of the wicked leads them astray.

27 The lazy do not roast any game, but the diligent feed on the riches of the hunt.

28 In the way of righteousness there is life; along that path is immortality.

Proverbs 12 - Prayer

Father, the more I read Your Word, the more I realize I need Your reproof. I have made a mess of things in my life along the way, and need Your correction to keep me on the path of righteousness. God, teach me to love Your correction. Don't let me settle for shallow living. If something in me needs to be called out–call it out. Burn away what's false. Sharpen what's dull. I want to grow.

I want to be a good person whose ways are pleasing to You and attract others to Your kingdom. I ask You to work in me by the power of Your Spirit to will and to do of Your good pleasure.

Help me to be diligent at my work today. Let me be faithful in the small things. Let me show up, keep going, and do the hard things even when no one's watching. Let my work be an offering to You–not just a way to pay the bills, but a way to bring life.

As I go about my day, I ask for Your wisdom as I plan and interact with my colleagues, bosses, subordinates, clients and prospective clients. I am thankful for my work, and want to do it with excellence.

You say that I will be "satisfied with good from the fruit of my words", and that my hard work will return to me as a blessing. Grant me the wisdom and power to guard my words and to work hard to excel at the work I have been given to do.

Let my words matter. Let them build, not break. Heal, not harm. Teach me to hold my tongue when silence is wisdom–and to speak when truth is needed. Your Word says reckless words pierce like swords–but the tongue of the wise brings healing. God, make me that man.

Lord, I know that anxiety is not from You and is a scheme of the enemy to get me to take my eyes off of You and Your sovereign plan for my life. Help me to speak words of peace and encouragement to those around me, dealing with anxiety and even to myself today.

Only by Your grace and the power of Your Spirit can I hope to walk in righteousness today. I ask that You help me walk with integrity today and experience the path of life.

What I'm hearing God say today:

PROVERBS 13

1 A wise son heeds his father's instruction, but a mocker does not respond to rebukes.

2 From the fruit of their lips people enjoy good things, but the unfaithful have an appetite for violence.

3 Those who guard their lips preserve their lives, but those who speak rashly will come to ruin.

4 A sluggard's appetite is never filled, but the desires of the diligent are fully satisfied.

5 The righteous hate what is false, but the wicked make themselves a stench and bring shame on themselves.

6 Righteousness guards the person of integrity, but wickedness overthrows the sinner.

7 One person pretends to be rich, yet has nothing; another pretends to be poor, yet has great wealth.

8 A person's riches may ransom their life, but the poor cannot respond to threatening rebukes.

9 The light of the righteous shines brightly, but the lamp of the wicked is snuffed out.

10 Where there is strife, there is pride, but wisdom is found in those who take advice.

11 Dishonest money dwindles away, but whoever gathers money little by little makes it grow.

12 Hope deferred makes the heart sick, but a longing fulfilled is a tree of life.

13 Whoever scorns instruction will pay for it, but whoever respects a command is rewarded.

14 The teaching of the wise is a fountain of life, turning a person from the snares of death.

15 Good judgment wins favor, but the way of the unfaithful leads to their destruction.

16 All who are prudent act with knowledge, but fools expose their folly.

17 A wicked messenger falls into trouble, but a trustworthy envoy brings healing.

18 Whoever disregards discipline comes to poverty and shame, but whoever heeds correction is honored.

19 A longing fulfilled is sweet to the soul, but fools detest turning from evil.

20 Walk with the wise and become wise, for a companion of fools suffers harm.

21 Trouble pursues the sinner, but the righteous are rewarded with good things.

22 A good person leaves an inheritance for their children's children, but a sinner's wealth is stored up for the righteous.

23 An unplowed field produces food for the poor, but injustice sweeps it away.

24 Whoever spares the rod hates their children, but the one who loves their children is careful to discipline them.

25 The righteous eat to their hearts' content, but the stomach of the wicked goes hungry.

Proverbs 13 - Prayer

Father, You remind me today that my speech, and my words are important. I will reap a harvest from what my mouth has sown, so it is crucial that I guard my words. When I have a tendency to be talkative or say too much, please govern my mouth to say only what is needed and what is guided by Your Spirit.

Teach me to guard my lips, Lord. Let my words carry weight, not wounds. Kill in me the need to always speak, always correct, always be right. Instead, teach me the strength of silence, and the wisdom of a word fitly spoken.

Help me to walk again today in the righteousness that Jesus provided me at the cross, and allow me to conduct myself with integrity in every situation I face.

Father, you remind me that financial wealth is gained by hard work and gathering "little by little" along the way. Help me to be patient and to trust You with my resources and financial future. Grant me the wisdom to steward well the resources You have already provided, and always remember that they are a gift and provision from Your hand.

I admit, Lord, that I can do nothing apart from You. I am desperate to hear Your instruction, direction, and insight today. Speak to me from Your Word and from other believers who are walking with You and hearing Your voice.

Help me to remain humble and continue to seek wise counsel. Help me also accept gracefully any correction and reproof You may need to speak to me along the way.

I ask that You surround me with wise, godly friends and help me avoid associating with those who walk in darkness.

Lead me, Lord, in my desire to leave an inheritance for my grandchildren. Help me to think through and plan wisely for the end-of-life issues that I know will arise when you call me home. In addition to finances, grant me wisdom and direction to be able to leave an inheritance to them of faithfulness, integrity, service, and Christian love.

What I'm hearing God say today:

PROVERBS 14

1 The wise woman builds her house, but with her own hands the foolish one tears hers down.

2 Whoever fears the LORD walks uprightly, but those who despise him are devious in their ways.

3 A fool's mouth lashes out with pride, but the lips of the wise protect them.

4 Where there are no oxen, the manger is empty, but from the strength of an ox come abundant harvests.

5 An honest witness does not deceive, but a false witness pours out lies.

6 The mocker seeks wisdom and finds none, but knowledge comes easily to the discerning.

7 Stay away from a fool, for you will not find knowledge on their lips.

8 The wisdom of the prudent is to give thought to their ways, but the folly of fools is deception.

9 Fools mock at making amends for sin, but goodwill is found among the upright.

10 Each heart knows its own bitterness, and no one else can share its joy.

11 The house of the wicked will be destroyed, but the tent of the upright will flourish.

12 There is a way that appears to be right, but in the end it leads to death.

13 Even in laughter the heart may ache, and rejoicing may end in grief.

14 The faithless will be fully repaid for their ways, and the good rewarded for theirs.

15 The simple believe anything, but the prudent give thought to their steps.

16 The wise fear the LORD and shun evil, but a fool is hotheaded and yet feels secure.

17 A quick-tempered person does foolish things, and the one who devises evil schemes is hated.

18 The simple inherit folly, but the prudent are crowned with knowledge.

19 Evildoers will bow down in the presence of the good, and the wicked at the gates of the righteous.

20 The poor are shunned even by their neighbors, but the rich have many friends.

21 It is a sin to despise one's neighbor, but blessed is the one who is kind to the needy.

22 Do not those who plot evil go astray? But those who plan what is good find love and faithfulness.

23 All hard work brings a profit, but mere talk leads only to poverty.

24 The wealth of the wise is their crown, but the folly of fools yields folly.

25 A truthful witness saves lives, but a false witness is deceitful.

26 Whoever fears the LORD has a secure fortress, and for their children it will be a refuge.

27 The fear of the LORD is a fountain of life, turning a person from the snares of death.

28 A large population is a king's glory, but without subjects a prince is ruined.

29 Whoever is patient has great understanding, but one who is quick-tempered displays folly.

30 A heart at peace gives life to the body, but envy rots the bones.

31 Whoever oppresses the poor shows contempt for their Maker, but whoever is kind to the needy honors God.

32 When calamity comes, the wicked are brought down, but even in death the righteous seek refuge in God.

33 Wisdom reposes in the heart of the discerning and even among fools she lets herself be known.

34 Righteousness exalts a nation, but sin condemns any people.

35 A king delights in a wise servant, but a shameful servant arouses his fury.

Proverbs 14 - Prayer

Father, help me walk in righteousness today and follow You closely. I am desperate to hear from You and to know what You would have me do today. Lord, I want to walk in honesty. Help me be consistent–living the same in private as I do in public. Let my choices reflect reverence for You.

Allow my speech to be true, life-giving, and filled with Your wisdom. Help me speak with gentleness and truth. Guard me from sarcasm, harshness, or careless words. Make my mouth a source of peace and life.

Grant me discernment in all my interactions today. I truly desire to walk uprightly today, Father, but I also know that I can't do that unless I stay close enough to You to hear Your voice and then choose to obey what You tell me to do.

Allow me, Lord, to turn away from evil of every kind, and to stay securely on the path You have laid out for me. I pray for discernment and for Your wise counsel to guide me.

I pray that You would fill my heart with compassion for the lost and less fortunate - and to be generous with the resources You have provided me.

I walk in fear and awe of You, Father, and am forever thankful that You chose me to be Your child and a joint heir with Jesus of Your kingdom. Thank You so much. In You I have strong confidence and will not be shaken.

I ask today that You grant me a tranquil heart as I lay all my cares at Your feet, Father. Thank You for being my fortress and my high tower against the enemy and the storms of life. I rest in Your love and Your sovereign plan for me today.

As I walk with You today, Lord, allow to me to be quick to hear, slow to speak and slow to anger. Align my thoughts with Yours and grant me patience in dealing with people today. Thank You that when I walk with You, I walk securely.

Today, I recommit to following You–step by step, decision by decision.

What I'm hearing God say today:

PROVERBS 15

1 A gentle answer turns away wrath, but a harsh word stirs up anger.

2 The tongue of the wise adorns knowledge, but the mouth of the fool gushes folly.

3 The eyes of the LORD are everywhere, keeping watch on the wicked and the good.

4 The soothing tongue is a tree of life, but a perverse tongue crushes the spirit.

5 A fool spurns a parent's discipline, but whoever heeds correction shows prudence.

6 The house of the righteous contains great treasure, but the income of the wicked brings ruin.

7 The lips of the wise spread knowledge, but the hearts of fools are not upright.

8 The LORD detests the sacrifice of the wicked, but the prayer of the upright pleases him.

9 The LORD detests the way of the wicked, but he loves those who pursue righteousness.

10 Stern discipline awaits anyone who leaves the path; the one who hates correction will die.

11 Death and Destruction lie open before the LORD – how much more do human hearts!

12 Mockers resent correction, so they avoid the wise.

13 A happy heart makes the face cheerful, but heartache crushes the spirit.

14 The discerning heart seeks knowledge, but the mouth of a fool feeds on folly.

15 All the days of the oppressed are wretched, but the cheerful heart has a continual feast.

16 Better a little with the fear of the LORD than great wealth with turmoil.

17 Better a small serving of vegetables with love than a fattened calf with hatred.

18 A hot-tempered person stirs up conflict, but the one who is patient calms a quarrel.

19 The way of the sluggard is blocked with thorns, but the path of the upright is a highway.

20 A wise son brings joy to his father, but a foolish man despises his mother.

21 Folly brings joy to one who has no sense, but whoever has understanding keeps a straight course.

22 Plans fail for lack of counsel, but with many advisers they succeed.

23 A person finds joy in giving an apt reply– and how good is a timely word!

24 The path of life leads upward for the prudent to keep them from going down to the realm of the dead.

25 The LORD tears down the house of the proud, but he sets the widow's boundary stones in place.

26 The LORD detests the thoughts of the wicked, but gracious words are pure in his sight.

27 The greedy bring ruin to their households, but the one who hates bribes will live.

28 The heart of the righteous weighs its answers, but the mouth of the wicked gushes evil.

29 The LORD is far from the wicked, but he hears the prayer of the righteous.

30 Light in a messenger's eyes brings joy to the heart, and good news gives health to the bones.

31 Whoever heeds life-giving correction will be at home among the wise.

32 Those who disregard discipline despise themselves, but the one who heeds correction gains understanding.

33 Wisdom's instruction is to fear the LORD, and humility comes before honor.

Proverbs 15 - Prayer

Father, I submit my words and my speech to You today and ask that they may be guided by Your Spirit. Allow me to offer gentle responses to people, full of wisdom and healing. When I'm frustrated or hurt, help me choose calm over conflict.

I earnestly seek to walk in righteousness today, Lord, and ask that You lead me in paths of righteousness for Your name's sake.

May my heart rejoice over Your mercy, forgiveness and love for me. May I be cheerful as I commune with You throughout this day - thankful to be chosen as Your beloved son and fellow heir with Jesus of the grace of life and Your eternal kingdom.

Father, I walk in awe of You, and ask that You continually fill my heart with praise and thanksgiving for Who You are and for all You have done.

May I be quick to listen to and love others well today. Allow me to be slow to anger and not easily provoked. May my speech and interactions with others bring honor to You today.

Would You raise up wise, Christian friends and mentors in my life that will assist me in making good decisions and righteousness plans, so that I may stay on the path You have established for me and walk in step with You. Allow me to use the resources and gifts You have given me to lead others to You and to bring You honor.

Father, everything I am and everything I have comes from You. I am humbled by Your generosity and grace, and ask that You allow me to walk in humility today and everyday - filled with thanksgiving in all things.

As Your son, I receive any correction or reproof that I need from You, in order to honor You with my life. Thank You for Your presence in me and with me today. I look forward to all You have in store for me.

What I'm hearing God say today:

PROVERBS 16

1 To humans belong the plans of the heart, but from the LORD comes the proper answer of the tongue.

2 All a person's ways seem pure to them, but motives are weighed by the LORD .

3 Commit to the LORD whatever you do, and he will establish your plans.

4 The LORD works out everything to its proper end– even the wicked for a day of disaster.

5 The LORD detests all the proud of heart. Be sure of this: They will not go unpunished.

6 Through love and faithfulness sin is atoned for; through the fear of the LORD evil is avoided.

7 When the LORD takes pleasure in anyone's way, he causes their enemies to make peace with them.

8 Better a little with righteousness than much gain with injustice.

9 In their hearts humans plan their course, but the LORD establishes their steps.

10 The lips of a king speak as an oracle, and his mouth does not betray justice.

11 Honest scales and balances belong to the LORD; all the weights in the bag are of his making.

12 Kings detest wrongdoing, for a throne is established through righteousness.

13 Kings take pleasure in honest lips; they value the one who speaks what is right.

14 A king's wrath is a messenger of death, but the wise will appease it.

15 When a king's face brightens, it means life; his favor is like a rain cloud in spring.

16 How much better to get wisdom than gold, to get insight rather than silver!

17 The highway of the upright avoids evil; those who guard their ways preserve their lives.

18 Pride goes before destruction, a haughty spirit before a fall.

19 Better to be lowly in spirit along with the oppressed than to share plunder with the proud.

20 Whoever gives heed to instruction prospers, and blessed is the one who trusts in the LORD .

21 The wise in heart are called discerning, and gracious words promote instruction.

22 Prudence is a fountain of life to the prudent, but folly brings punishment to fools.

23 The hearts of the wise make their mouths prudent, and their lips promote instruction.

24 Gracious words are a honeycomb, sweet to the soul and healing to the bones.

25 There is a way that appears to be right, but in the end it leads to death.

26 The appetite of laborers works for them; their hunger drives them on.

27 A scoundrel plots evil, and on their lips it is like a scorching fire.

28 A perverse person stirs up conflict, and a gossip separates close friends.

29 A violent person entices their neighbor and leads them down a path that is not good.

30 Whoever winks with their eye is plotting perversity; whoever purses their lips is bent on evil.

31 Gray hair is a crown of splendor; it is attained in the way of righteousness.

32 Better a patient person than a warrior, one with self-control than one who takes a city.

33 The lot is cast into the lap, but its every decision is from the LORD .

Proverbs 16 - Prayer

Father, I bring all my plans and all my motives before You today. I submit to Your wisdom and direction concerning my calendar, my "to-do" list, and even my unspoken hopes and dreams that You already know, I'm sure. I surrender my agenda. I want Your answers, Your timing, Your will.

As You direct my steps today, please help me avoid evil influences and walk in Your unconditional love, mercy and truth. May my ways be pleasing to You.

Allow me to reject thoughts of selfishness and pride today, to remain humble before You, and put the needs of others ahead of my own. Refine my motives. Burn away the hypocrisy. Make me clean on the inside.

Father, please grant me wisdom and discernment today. I need Your insight regarding the opportunities and the difficulties I will face. Speak loudly please and give me ears to hear.

Strengthen me today to be slow to anger, and be quick to love, forgive and grant grace to others You place in my path. Thank You that You are continuing to chisel away at my flesh and mold me into the man You need me to be.

Thank You that You reign today! You are working sovereignly in my life and through my circumstances and relationships - and I am grateful.

Lord, shepherd me today. Keep me close enough to You to hear Your voice, and give me the courage to follow You wherever You lead - knowing that You will only lead me in paths of righteousness for Your name's sake, and for my best good.

Keep me from feeling that I know best, and that my way is the best way. I reject any thoughts or feelings of independence. I desire to stay close behind You and follow your lead. You are the Good Shepherd, and I completely trust where You are leading me. Thank You for Your patience and mercy, and for Your never-ending love.

What I'm hearing God say today:

PROVERBS 17

1 Better a dry crust with peace and quiet than a house full of feasting, with strife.

2 A prudent servant will rule over a disgraceful son and will share the inheritance as one of the family.

3 The crucible for silver and the furnace for gold, but the LORD tests the heart.

4 A wicked person listens to deceitful lips; a liar pays attention to a destructive tongue.

5 Whoever mocks the poor shows contempt for their Maker; whoever gloats over disaster will not go unpunished.

6 Children's children are a crown to the aged, and parents are the pride of their children.

7 Eloquent lips are unsuited to a godless fool— how much worse lying lips to a ruler!

8 A bribe is seen as a charm by the one who gives it; they think success will come at every turn.

9 Whoever would foster love covers over an offense, but whoever repeats the matter separates close friends.

10 A rebuke impresses a discerning person more than a hundred lashes a fool.

11 Evildoers foster rebellion against God; the messenger of death will be sent against them.

12 Better to meet a bear robbed of her cubs than a fool bent on folly.

13 Evil will never leave the house of one who pays back evil for good.

14 Starting a quarrel is like breaching a dam; so drop the matter before a dispute breaks out.

15 Acquitting the guilty and condemning the innocent– the LORD detests them both.

16 Why should fools have money in hand to buy wisdom, when they are not able to understand it?

17 A friend loves at all times, and a brother is born for a time of adversity.

18 One who has no sense shakes hands in pledge and puts up security for a neighbor.

19 Whoever loves a quarrel loves sin; whoever builds a high gate invites destruction.

20 One whose heart is corrupt does not prosper; one whose tongue is perverse falls into trouble.

21 To have a fool for a child brings grief; there is no joy for the parent of a godless fool.

22 A cheerful heart is good medicine, but a crushed spirit dries up the bones.

23 The wicked accept bribes in secret to pervert the course of justice.

24 A discerning person keeps wisdom in view, but a fool's eyes wander to the ends of the earth.

25 A foolish son brings grief to his father and bitterness to the mother who bore him.

26 If imposing a fine on the innocent is not good, surely to flog honest officials is not right.

27 The one who has knowledge uses words with restraint, and whoever has understanding is even-tempered.

28 Even fools are thought wise if they keep silent, and discerning if they hold their tongues.

Proverbs 17 - Prayer

Father, may my heart be pleasing to You when You test it. Help me to guard my heart above all else, because everything I do flows from it. I submit my thoughts, words, and actions "to You" today, Lord.

May I have a heart that loves others, as You have loved me, and also forgives others as I have been forgiven by You. Help me never repay evil for good and may I quickly avoid strife as it arises in my day.

I thank You today for my children and the crown of grandchildren. They are a blessing from You, and Your instruments to teach me and grow me up into the man I need to be.

Help me, Lord, to avoid quarrels and to drop a matter before it escalates into an argument. Give me grace to be a friend who loves at all times and in every situation. Thank You for my close friends and brothers in Christ. Bless them abundantly today and protect them as they seek to walk closely with You.

Grant me a cheerful heart today, Lord, as I cast all my cares and burdens upon You, and remind me to trust in the good plans You have for me.

Because Your Spirit lives in me, I have everything I need today. Thank You that You promise to meet all my needs through Your riches in Christ Jesus.

Guide me by Your wisdom and discernment throughout this day. May I guard my words and remain calm in the midst of conflict. I again submit my thoughts, words and actions today, Lord.

May my words bring life and grace today and not death and discouragement. Remind me to hold my tongue if I have no gracious words to speak. Fill my heart with love and grace instead of anger and division.

Open my eyes for opportunities to be generous to others and to walk in humility before You. Counsel me, Father, as I seek to honor You with my life today.

What I'm hearing God say today:

PROVERBS 18

1 An unfriendly person pursues selfish ends and against all sound judgment starts quarrels.

2 Fools find no pleasure in understanding but delight in airing their own opinions.

3 When wickedness comes, so does contempt, and with shame comes reproach.

4 The words of the mouth are deep waters, but the fountain of wisdom is a rushing stream.

5 It is not good to be partial to the wicked and so deprive the innocent of justice.

6 The lips of fools bring them strife, and their mouths invite a beating.

7 The mouths of fools are their undoing, and their lips are a snare to their very lives.

8 The words of a gossip are like choice morsels; they go down to the inmost parts.

9 One who is slack in his work is brother to one who destroys.

10 The name of the LORD is a fortified tower; the righteous run to it and are safe.

11 The wealth of the rich is their fortified city; they imagine it a wall too high to scale.

12 Before a downfall the heart is haughty, but humility comes before honor.

13 To answer before listening– that is folly and shame.

14 The human spirit can endure in sickness, but a crushed spirit who can bear?

15 The heart of the discerning acquires knowledge, for the ears of the wise seek it out.

16 A gift opens the way and ushers the giver into the presence of the great.

17 In a lawsuit the first to speak seems right, until someone comes forward and cross-examines.

18 Casting the lot settles disputes and keeps strong opponents apart.

19 A brother wronged is more unyielding than a fortified city; disputes are like the barred gates of a citadel.

20 From the fruit of their mouth a person's stomach is filled; with the harvest of their lips they are satisfied.

21 The tongue has the power of life and death, and those who love it will eat its fruit.

22 He who finds a wife finds what is good and receives favor from the LORD.

23 The poor plead for mercy, but the rich answer harshly.

24 One who has unreliable friends soon comes to ruin, but there is a friend who sticks closer than a brother.

Proverbs 18 - Prayer

Father, I seek Your wisdom and understanding today. Help me surround myself with faithful, God-fearing friends who speak life and sound wisdom to me.

Continue to guard my lips that I may speak words of truth and life to those around me. Keep me from gossip and all foolish talk.

Thank You that Your name is the name above all names and every knee in heaven and earth bows before the name of Jesus.

Your name is my refuge and my strong tower against the forces of darkness. Thank You that You have granted me authority to invoke Your name in battle against our enemy.

Help me to avoid pride today, Lord, and walk in humility before You. Keep me from answering someone before fully listening to their heart and not simply their words.

While I long for Your wisdom and discernment, I seek Your presence above all. Help me to follow You closely today, to hear Your voice, and follow Your leadership.

Thank You for the gifts, talents and abilities You have given me. I submit all of them to Your leadership and Lordship, and ask that You allow me to use them today to glorify You and to lead others to You.

Guard my tongue today and help me to speak life-giving words that lift others up and bring them encouragement.

Thank You so much for the gift of a good wife. Work in me today to love her as You love me, and to lay my life down for her like You did for me. I am naturally selfish, Lord, and I need You to empower me to place her needs above my own and to make her my top priority today.

Lord, would you help me be a loyal and true friend? Help me be supportive, reliable and available to my friends, and to love and serve them well.

What I'm hearing God say today:

PROVERBS 19

1 Better the poor whose walk is blameless than a fool whose lips are perverse.

2 Desire without knowledge is not good— how much more will hasty feet miss the way!

3 A person's own folly leads to their ruin, yet their heart rages against the LORD .

4 Wealth attracts many friends, but even the closest friend of the poor person deserts them.

5 A false witness will not go unpunished, and whoever pours out lies will not go free.

6 Many curry favor with a ruler, and everyone is the friend of one who gives gifts.

7 The poor are shunned by all their relatives— how much more do their friends avoid them! Though the poor pursue them with pleading, they are nowhere to be found.

8 The one who gets wisdom loves life; the one who cherishes understanding will soon prosper.

9 A false witness will not go unpunished, and whoever pours out lies will perish.

10 It is not fitting for a fool to live in luxury— how much worse for a slave to rule over princes!

11 A person's wisdom yields patience; it is to one's glory to overlook an offense.

12 A king's rage is like the roar of a lion, but his favor is like dew on the grass.

13 A foolish child is a father's ruin, and a quarrelsome wife is like the constant dripping of a leaky roof.

14 Houses and wealth are inherited from parents, but a prudent wife is from the LORD .

15 Laziness brings on deep sleep, and the shiftless go hungry.

16 Whoever keeps commandments keeps their life, but whoever shows contempt for their ways will die.

17 Whoever is kind to the poor lends to the LORD, and he will reward them for what they have done.

18 Discipline your children, for in that there is hope; do not be a willing party to their death.

19 A hot-tempered person must pay the penalty; rescue them, and you will have to do it again.

20 Listen to advice and accept discipline, and at the end you will be counted among the wise.

21 Many are the plans in a person's heart, but it is the LORD 's purpose that prevails.

22 What a person desires is unfailing love; better to be poor than a liar.

23 The fear of the LORD leads to life; then one rests content, untouched by trouble.

24 A sluggard buries his hand in the dish; he will not even bring it back to his mouth!

25 Flog a mocker, and the simple will learn prudence; rebuke the discerning, and they will gain knowledge.

26 Whoever robs their father and drives out their mother is a child who brings shame and disgrace.

27 Stop listening to instruction, my son, and you will stray from the words of knowledge.

28 A corrupt witness mocks at justice, and the mouth of the wicked gulps down evil.

29 Penalties are prepared for mockers, and beatings for the backs of fools.

Proverbs 19 - Prayer

Empower me today, Lord, to walk with integrity, to speak the truth with love and to be upright in all my interactions with people.

Allow me to be cheerfully generous with the time, talent and resources you give me.

I long to gain wisdom and good sense, and to walk with understanding in all my ways. Grant me the grace to overlook any offenses against me and to be slow to anger and quick to forgive.

Encourage me to be diligent in my work and to do my work as unto You. Help me be generous to others in need, especially to my brothers and sisters in Christ.

Grant me Your wisdom in dealing with my children. Guide me in administering loving , appropriate discipline, and instruction.

May I also receive discipline from You with grace, knowing that You love me and only want the best for me.

I am desperate for Your counsel as I make my plans. Help me not presume on Your grace and to involve You in my goals and plans.

You say that "what is desirable in a man is his loyalty and unfailing love". Would You help me to be such man, Lord?

The fear of the Lord leads to life, so that one may sleep satisfied, untouched by evil. - Proverbs 19:23

What I'm hearing God say today:

PROVERBS 20

1 Wine is a mocker and beer a brawler; whoever is led astray by them is not wise.

2 A king's wrath strikes terror like the roar of a lion; those who anger him forfeit their lives.

3 It is to one's honor to avoid strife, but every fool is quick to quarrel.

4 Sluggards do not plow in season; so at harvest time they look but find nothing.

5 The purposes of a person's heart are deep waters, but one who has insight draws them out.

6 Many claim to have unfailing love, but a faithful person who can find?

7 The righteous lead blameless lives; blessed are their children after them.

8 When a king sits on his throne to judge, he winnows out all evil with his eyes.

9 Who can say, "I have kept my heart pure; I am clean and without sin"?

10 Differing weights and differing measures— the LORD detests them both.

11 Even small children are known by their actions, so is their conduct really pure and upright?

12 Ears that hear and eyes that see— the LORD has made them both.

13 Do not love sleep or you will grow poor; stay awake and you will have food to spare.

14 "It's no good, it's no good!" says the buyer— then goes off and boasts about the purchase.

15 Gold there is, and rubies in abundance, but lips that speak knowledge are a rare jewel.

16 Take the garment of one who puts up security for a stranger; hold it in pledge if it is done for an outsider.

17 Food gained by fraud tastes sweet, but one ends up with a mouth full of gravel.

18 Plans are established by seeking advice; so if you wage war, obtain guidance.

19 A gossip betrays a confidence; so avoid anyone who talks too much.

20 If someone curses their father or mother, their lamp will be snuffed out in pitch darkness.

21 An inheritance claimed too soon will not be blessed at the end.

22 Do not say, "I'll pay you back for this wrong!" Wait for the LORD, and he will avenge you.

23 The LORD detests differing weights, and dishonest scales do not please him.

24 A person's steps are directed by the LORD . How then can anyone understand their own way?

25 It is a trap to dedicate something rashly and only later to consider one's vows.

26 A wise king winnows out the wicked; he drives the threshing wheel over them.

27 The human spirit is [a] the lamp of the LORD that sheds light on one's inmost being.

28 Love and faithfulness keep a king safe; through love his throne is made secure.

29 The glory of young men is their strength, gray hair the splendor of the old.

30 Blows and wounds scrub away evil, and beatings purge the inmost being.

Proverbs 20 - Prayer

Father, keep me from strife and quarrels today. Allow me to walk with integrity in all my ways and be faithful in all my dealings with people today. May my actions and interactions be pure and right in Your eyes.

Help me be diligent and hard working in my career, Lord. May I do whatever work I am given with my whole heart and to Your glory.

Lord, I want to be the "righteous man who walks in integrity and lives life according to Godly beliefs". I long for Your blessing on my children and my children's children. May I be an example of a man who makes You his top priority and knows You intimately.

Help my ears to hear what You're speaking to me today. Open my eyes to see how You are working in and around me, and allow me to be an active participant in what You're doing.

Guide me to wise counsel as I make plans for the future and please continue to guide my steps. Speak to me through Your Word and through prayer, Father.

Keep me from vengeful thoughts and actions when someone offends me, and help me entrust them to You.

Help me to deal honestly and truthfully with those I interact with today. Guide me with integrity in all my ways.

Since You are the Creator of the hearing ear and the seeing eye, Father, please bless me with both. I so want to hear Your voice above all other voices, and I walk in complete darkness unless You grant me eyes that see.

Keep me from gossip and flattery today. Allow me to speak the truth in love and be trustworthy with information shared with me.

Lord, use Your lamp to search and examine my innermost parts. Reveal any wicked way in me so that I can quickly repent and renounce it - and return to the joy of Your presence.

What I'm hearing God say today:

PROVERBS 21

1 In the LORD's hand the king's heart is a stream of water that he channels toward all who please him.

2 A person may think their own ways are right, but the LORD weighs the heart.

3 To do what is right and just is more acceptable to the LORD than sacrifice.

4 Haughty eyes and a proud heart– the unplowed field of the wicked–produce sin.

5 The plans of the diligent lead to profit as surely as haste leads to poverty.

6 A fortune made by a lying tongue is a fleeting vapor and a deadly snare. [a]

7 The violence of the wicked will drag them away, for they refuse to do what is right.

8 The way of the guilty is devious, but the conduct of the innocent is upright.

9 Better to live on a corner of the roof than share a house with a quarrelsome wife.

10 The wicked crave evil; their neighbors get no mercy from them.

11 When a mocker is punished, the simple gain wisdom; by paying attention to the wise they get knowledge.

12 The Righteous One takes note of the house of the wicked and brings the wicked to ruin.

13 Whoever shuts their ears to the cry of the poor will also cry out and not be answered.

14 A gift given in secret soothes anger, and a bribe concealed in the cloak pacifies great wrath.

15 When justice is done, it brings joy to the righteous but terror to evildoers.

16 Whoever strays from the path of prudence comes to rest in the company of the dead.

17 Whoever loves pleasure will become poor; whoever loves wine and olive oil will never be rich.

18 The wicked become a ransom for the righteous, and the unfaithful for the upright.

19 Better to live in a desert than with a quarrelsome and nagging wife.

20 The wise store up choice food and olive oil, but fools gulp theirs down.

21 Whoever pursues righteousness and love finds life, prosperity and honor.

22 One who is wise can go up against the city of the mighty and pull down the stronghold in which they trust.

23 Those who guard their mouths and their tongues keep themselves from calamity.

24 The proud and arrogant person—"Mocker" is his name— behaves with insolent fury.

25 The craving of a sluggard will be the death of him, because his hands refuse to work.

26 All day long he craves for more, but the righteous give without sparing.

27 The sacrifice of the wicked is detestable– how much more so when brought with evil intent!

28 A false witness will perish, but a careful listener will testify successfully.

29 The wicked put up a bold front, but the upright give thought to their ways.

30 There is no wisdom, no insight, no plan that can succeed against the LORD.

31 The horse is made ready for the day of battle, but victory rests with the LORD

Proverbs 21 - Prayer

Father, forgive me when I think my way is the best way and justify wandering away from You in order to follow the path I think is right. My heart longs to follow You and the plans You have for me. Thank You for Your mercy and long-suffering with me.

Allow me to treat the people around me with integrity and mercy, and not think of myself more highly than I should. Please guard my heart from pride today.

Help me to do what You call me to do today with excellence, without compromise or cutting corners. I want to represent You well in my workplace, Lord, and influence those around me for Your kingdom.

Father, please guard my household from contention and strife. I ask You to bless my marriage and my family relationships with unity, love and peace.

Help me to have a heart overflowing with generosity today, as You have been so abundantly generous with me. Show me how I can bless those less fortunate than me, and grant me wisdom to discern those who truly need a blessing from You.

Thank You, Lord, for the internal peace and genuine joy You give me when I am walking daily with You. Help me to walk in step with You today, to hear Your voice clearly, and to gladly respond to Your instruction.

I thank You also for the abundant provision You have blessed me with. Help me to never love "things" or look to them for pleasure and satisfaction instead of You. Help me to be a wise steward of what You have provided, and to never place my trust in Your provision over You.

I desire to walk with You in righteousness today, Lord. Help me to consider my ways and submit my plans, goals, and agendas to You and Your Lordship.

Thank You for establishing my way today. I walk in victory today because I walk with You.

What I'm hearing God say today:

PROVERBS 22

1 A good name is more desirable than great riches; to be esteemed is better than silver or gold.

2 Rich and poor have this in common: The LORD is the Maker of them all.

3 The prudent see danger and take refuge, but the simple keep going and pay the penalty.

4 Humility is the fear of the LORD ; its wages are riches and honor and life.

5 In the paths of the wicked are snares and pitfalls, but those who would preserve their life stay far from them.

6 Start children off on the way they should go, and even when they are old they will not turn from it.

7 The rich rule over the poor, and the borrower is slave to the lender.

8 Whoever sows injustice reaps calamity, and the rod they wield in fury will be broken.

9 The generous will themselves be blessed, for they share their food with the poor.

10 Drive out the mocker, and out goes strife; quarrels and insults are ended.

11 One who loves a pure heart and who speaks with grace will have the king for a friend.

12 The eyes of the LORD keep watch over knowledge, but he frustrates the words of the unfaithful.

13 The sluggard says, "There's a lion outside! I'll be killed in the public square!"

14 The mouth of an adulterous woman is a deep pit; a man who is under the LORD's wrath falls into it.

15 Folly is bound up in the heart of a child, but the rod of discipline will drive it far away.

16 One who oppresses the poor to increase his wealth and one who gives gifts to the rich—both come to poverty.

Thirty Sayings of the Wise Saying 1

17 Pay attention and turn your ear to the sayings of the wise; apply your heart to what I teach,

18 for it is pleasing when you keep them in your heart and have all of them ready on your lips.

19 So that your trust may be in the LORD, I teach you today, even you.

20 Have I not written thirty sayings for you, sayings of counsel and knowledge,

21 teaching you to be honest and to speak the truth, so that you bring back truthful reports to those you serve?

Saying 2

22 Do not exploit the poor because they are poor and do not crush the needy in court,

23 for the LORD will take up their case and will exact life for life.

Saying 3

24 Do not make friends with a hot-tempered person, do not associate with one easily angered,

25 or you may learn their ways and get yourself ensnared.

Saying 4

26 Do not be one who shakes hands in pledge or puts up security for debts;

27 if you lack the means to pay, your very bed will be snatched from under you.

Saying 5

28 Do not move an ancient boundary stone set up by your ancestors.

Saying 6

29 Do you see someone skilled in their work? They will serve before kings; they will not serve before officials of low rank.

Proverbs 22 - Prayer

Father, grant that I would live in such a manner as to have a good name and good favor as I seek to glorify You and make You known. Develop moral courage and integrity in me that my behavior would be honorable to You.

Help me to be discerning and purposeful regarding the ever-present battle with evil and sin. Allow me to walk alertly and in full awareness of the enemy's schemes. Thank You for the authority, armor and weapons You have given me in order to overcome the enemy.

Father, everything I am and everything I have comes from You. I am so very grateful for Your love, Your forgiveness, and Your generosity. Without You I can do nothing, and I am humbled to remember You chose me, died for me, and adopted me into Your family and eternal kingdom.

Help me, Lord, to be deliberate in taking whatever time necessary with my children to train them up in Your Word and Your ways. Help me encourage them to always seek Your wisdom and will for how to best use their abilities and talents to glorify You.

Help me also, Lord, to have divine wisdom regarding how to best discipline my children. As You discipline me out of Your great love for me, help me also not shrink from disciplining my children in order to drive foolishness from them.

Allow me opportunities to be generous with my time, my gifts and my resources as You lead me along righteous paths.

Help me today to incline my ears to listen carefully to Your Word and to apply what You are teaching me. Allow me to keep Your Words in my heart and on my lips, so that my trust and confidence may be in You alone.

What I'm hearing God say today:

PROVERBS 23

Saying 7

1 When you sit to dine with a ruler, note well what [a] is before you,

2 and put a knife to your throat if you are given to gluttony.

3 Do not crave his delicacies, for that food is deceptive.

Saying 8

4 Do not wear yourself out to get rich; do not trust your own cleverness.

5 Cast but a glance at riches, and they are gone, for they will surely sprout wings and fly off to the sky like an eagle.

Saying 9

6 Do not eat the food of a begrudging host, do not crave his delicacies;

7 for he is the kind of person who is always thinking about the cost. [b] "Eat and drink," he says to you, but his heart is not with you.

8 You will vomit up the little you have eaten and will have wasted your compliments.

Saying 10

9 Do not speak to fools, for they will scorn your prudent words.

Saying 11

10 Do not move an ancient boundary stone or encroach on the fields of the fatherless,

11 for their Defender is strong; he will take up their case against you.

Saying 12

12 Apply your heart to instruction and your ears to words of knowledge.

Saying 13

13 Do not withhold discipline from a child; if you punish them with the rod, they will not die.

14 Punish them with the rod and save them from death.

Saying 14

15 My son, if your heart is wise, then my heart will be glad indeed;

16 my inmost being will rejoice when your lips speak what is right.

Saying 15

17 Do not let your heart envy sinners, but always be zealous for the fear of the LORD .

18 There is surely a future hope for you, and your hope will not be cut off.

Saying 16

19 Listen, my son, and be wise, and set your heart on the right path:

20 Do not join those who drink too much wine or gorge themselves on meat,

21 for drunkards and gluttons become poor, and drowsiness clothes them in rags.

Saying 17

22 Listen to your father, who gave you life, and do not despise your mother when she is old.

23 Buy the truth and do not sell it— wisdom, instruction and insight as well.

24 The father of a righteous child has great joy; a man who fathers a wise son rejoices in him.

25 May your father and mother rejoice; may she who gave you birth be joyful!

Saying 18

26 My son, give me your heart and let your eyes delight in my ways,

27 for an adulterous woman is a deep pit, and a wayward wife is a narrow well.

28 Like a bandit she lies in wait and multiplies the unfaithful among men.

Saying 19

29 Who has woe? Who has sorrow? Who has strife? Who has complaints? Who has needless bruises? Who has bloodshot eyes?

30 Those who linger over wine, who go to sample bowls of mixed wine.

31 Do not gaze at wine when it is red, when it sparkles in the cup, when it goes down smoothly!

32 In the end it bites like a snake and poisons like a viper.

33 Your eyes will see strange sights, and your mind will imagine confusing things.

34 You will be like one sleeping on the high seas, lying on top of the rigging.

35 "They hit me," you will say, "but I'm not hurt! They beat me, but I don't feel it! When will I wake up so I can find another drink?"

Proverbs 23 - Prayer

Father, the American dream is to accumulate wealth over time in order to enjoy a leisurely retirement. I ask that You help me to not make wealth an idol or my primary goal in life - for wealth, without You is meaningless. Help me to focus on following You, working hard, saving wisely and trusting You with my financial future.

Remind me today that I will become what I think in my heart. I want to agree with who Your Word says I am and not believe the deception and lies of the enemy. I am a forgiven, adopted son of the King of all Kings. I am deeply loved. I am significant. I am worthy. I am royalty.

Thank You for another reminder that discipline is good for my children, and withholding it is unwise and unloving.

Help me to gain Godly wisdom as I walk with You today. Allow me to speak wise and righteous things, to never envy the lives of sinners, and to live in reverent fear of You.

Thank You that my future is secure and my hope and expectation rest in Your unfailing love and sovereign plan for me.

Direct my heart today, Father, to follow Your ways. Instruct me, Lord, in Your truth and fill my heart with Your wisdom and understanding.

I give you my heart, Lord, and eagerly follow where You are leading. Help me hear Your voice clearly and have the courage to follow Your leading.
The allure of sin is ever-present with me. The voices of sin, adultery, pornography, addiction, and compromise shout from every street corner it seems.

Empower me, Lord, to resist turning aside to hear their temptations and ponder their lies. Keep me on Your path today, and help me stay focused on the blessings ahead as I follow You.

What I'm hearing God say today:

PROVERBS 24

Saying 20

1 Do not envy the wicked, do not desire their company;

2 for their hearts plot violence, and their lips talk about making trouble.

Saying 21

3 By wisdom a house is built, and through understanding it is established;

4 through knowledge its rooms are filled with rare and beautiful treasures.

Saying 22

5 The wise prevail through great power, and those who have knowledge muster their strength.

6 Surely you need guidance to wage war, and victory is won through many advisers.

Saying 23

7 Wisdom is too high for fools; in the assembly at the gate they must not open their mouths.

Saying 24

8 Whoever plots evil will be known as a schemer.

9 The schemes of folly are sin, and people detest a mocker.

Saying 25

10 If you falter in a time of trouble, how small is your strength!

11 Rescue those being led away to death; hold back those staggering toward slaughter.

12 If you say, "But we knew nothing about this," does not he who weighs the heart perceive it? Does not he who guards your life know it? Will he not repay everyone according to what they have done?

Saying 26

13 Eat honey, my son, for it is good; honey from the comb is sweet to your taste.

14 Know also that wisdom is like honey for you: If you find it, there is a future hope for you, and your hope will not be cut off.

Saying 27

15 Do not lurk like a thief near the house of the righteous, do not plunder their dwelling place;

16 for though the righteous fall seven times, they rise again, but the wicked stumble when calamity strikes.

Saying 28

17 Do not gloat when your enemy falls; when they stumble, do not let your heart rejoice,

18 or the LORD will see and disapprove and turn his wrath away from them.

Saying 29

19 Do not fret because of evildoers or be envious of the wicked,

20 for the evildoer has no future hope, and the lamp of the wicked will be snuffed out.

Saying 30

21 Fear the LORD and the king, my son, and do not join with rebellious officials,

22 for those two will send sudden destruction on them, and who knows what calamities they can bring?

Further Sayings of the Wise

23 These also are sayings of the wise: To show partiality in judging is not good:

24 Whoever says to the guilty, "You are innocent," will be cursed by peoples and denounced by nations.

25 But it will go well with those who convict the guilty, and rich blessing will come on them.

26 An honest answer is like a kiss on the lips.

27 Put your outdoor work in order and get your fields ready; after that, build your house.

28 Do not testify against your neighbor without cause– would you use your lips to mislead?

29 Do not say, "I'll do to them as they have done to me; I'll pay them back for what they did."

30 I went past the field of a sluggard, past the vineyard of someone who has no sense;

31 thorns had come up everywhere, the ground was covered with weeds, and the stone wall was in ruins.

32 I applied my heart to what I observed and learned a lesson from what I saw:

33 A little sleep, a little slumber, a little folding of the hands to rest–

34 and poverty will come on you like a thief and scarcity like an armed man.

Proverbs 24 - Prayer

Father, keep me from ever envying evil people. Sometimes what they have and what they do seem attractive, but I know it is all a trap of the enemy. I desire what You have for me, Lord, and know I will never lack the things I need or the things that bring abundant life as Your child.

I ask again today for Your wisdom and understanding. Speak to me from Your Word and by Your Spirit inside me, and allow me to have ears to hear and a heart to follow.

Help me to walk as a wise warrior today, protected by Your armor, wielding the sword of Your Word with precision. You have given me Your authority and divinely powerful weapons to defeat every scheme of the enemy and to demolish his strongholds.

Thank You that You guard my life and repay everyone according to their deeds. May my deeds be the result of walking in Your presence and obeying Your voice.

Thank You that You are the author of wisdom - and all wisdom resides with You and comes from You. By Your wisdom I have a future and a hope as I follow and listen to You.

When I fall You are there to pick me up and teach me from my mistakes. You forgive me when I confess my sin and repent. Thank You for Your great mercy and long-suffering towards me. I will not listen to the enemy's accusations of guilt, shame, and rejection - but, rather I will repent and walk in freedom and victory as Your child.

Help me not to be jealous or covet the success of evil people, but to place my life plans and my success completely in Your hands.

May I work diligently today at everything I have to do. My work, my career, my boss, my colleagues, and my clients are all part of Your divine plan for my life right now, and I want to honor You by my work ethic and my treatment of those around me. Lead me today, Father.

What I'm hearing God say today:

PROVERBS 25

1 These are more proverbs of Solomon, compiled by the men of Hezekiah king of Judah:

2 It is the glory of God to conceal a matter; to search out a matter is the glory of kings.

3 As the heavens are high and the earth is deep, so the hearts of kings are unsearchable.

4 Remove the dross from the silver, and a silversmith can produce a vessel;

5 remove wicked officials from the king's presence, and his throne will be established through righteousness.

6 Do not exalt yourself in the king's presence, and do not claim a place among his great men;

7 it is better for him to say to you, "Come up here," than for him to humiliate you before his nobles. What you have seen with your eyes

8 do not bring hastily to court, for what will you do in the end if your neighbor puts you to shame?

9 If you take your neighbor to court, do not betray another's confidence,

10 or the one who hears it may shame you and the charge against you will stand.

11 Like apples of gold in settings of silver is a ruling rightly given.

12 Like an earring of gold or an ornament of fine gold is the rebuke of a wise judge to a listening ear.

13 Like a snow-cooled drink at harvest time is a trustworthy messenger to the one who sends him; he refreshes the spirit of his master.

14 Like clouds and wind without rain is one who boasts of gifts never given.

15 Through patience a ruler can be persuaded, and a gentle tongue can break a bone.

16 If you find honey, eat just enough— too much of it, and you will vomit.

17 Seldom set foot in your neighbor's house— too much of you, and they will hate you.

18 Like a club or a sword or a sharp arrow is one who gives false testimony against a neighbor.

19 Like a broken tooth or a lame foot is reliance on the unfaithful in a time of trouble.

20 Like one who takes away a garment on a cold day, or like vinegar poured on a wound, is one who sings songs to a heavy heart.

21 If your enemy is hungry, give him food to eat; if he is thirsty, give him water to drink.

22 In doing this, you will heap burning coals on his head, and the LORD will reward you.

23 Like a north wind that brings unexpected rain is a sly tongue—which provokes a horrified look.

24 Better to live on a corner of the roof than share a house with a quarrelsome wife.

25 Like cold water to a weary soul is good news from a distant land.

26 Like a muddied spring or a polluted well are the righteous who give way to the wicked.

27 It is not good to eat too much honey, nor is it honorable to search out matters that are too deep.

28 Like a city whose walls are broken through is a person who lacks self-control.

Proverbs 25 - Prayer

Father, help me to walk with You in humility today, remembering to put the needs of others above my own. Keep me from pride and thinking more highly of myself than I should.

Guard my mouth and allow my words to be filled with wisdom, grace and truth. Grant me discernment and grace in my daily interactions with family, friends, colleagues and neighbors - knowing that I represent You wherever I go.

Work in me, Lord, to be known as a trustworthy and faithful man. Help me to avoid gossip or slander in any way today, and allow me to safeguard the private news and information of others.

Grant me grace to truly forgive those who have offended or harmed me in any way, and to be willing to bless them instead of becoming bitter and resentful.

Help my focus today be to live in such a way as to bring You glory and not to seek my own glory. Anything worthy of praise in my life is only the result of You working in and through me, so I can take no credit for myself.

Father, when people and circumstances upset me, help me control my anger and my reactions. Help me to always remember that I am Your child, and a joint heir with Jesus of Your kingdom. Give me the grace to respond well when I am under pressure or confronted by difficulty.

Good sense and discretion make a man slow to anger, and it is to his honor and glory to overlook a transgression or an offense.   Proverbs 19:11

What I'm hearing God say today:

PROVERBS 26

1 Like snow in summer or rain in harvest, honor is not fitting for a fool.

2 Like a fluttering sparrow or a darting swallow, an undeserved curse does not come to rest.

3 A whip for the horse, a bridle for the donkey, and a rod for the backs of fools!

4 Do not answer a fool according to his folly, or you yourself will be just like him.

5 Answer a fool according to his folly, or he will be wise in his own eyes.

6 Sending a message by the hands of a fool is like cutting off one's feet or drinking poison.

7 Like the useless legs of one who is lame is a proverb in the mouth of a fool.

8 Like tying a stone in a sling is the giving of honor to a fool.

9 Like a thornbush in a drunkard's hand is a proverb in the mouth of a fool.

10 Like an archer who wounds at random is one who hires a fool or any passer-by.

11 As a dog returns to its vomit, so fools repeat their folly.

12 Do you see a person wise in their own eyes? There is more hope for a fool than for them.

13 A sluggard says, "There's a lion in the road, a fierce lion roaming the streets!"

14 As a door turns on its hinges, so a sluggard turns on his bed.

15 A sluggard buries his hand in the dish; he is too lazy to bring it back to his mouth.

16 A sluggard is wiser in his own eyes than seven people who answer discreetly.

17 Like one who grabs a stray dog by the ears is someone who rushes into a quarrel not their own.

18 Like a maniac shooting flaming arrows of death

19 is one who deceives their neighbor and says, "I was only joking!"

20 Without wood a fire goes out; without a gossip a quarrel dies down.

21 As charcoal to embers and as wood to fire, so is a quarrelsome person for kindling strife.

22 The words of a gossip are like choice morsels; they go down to the inmost parts.

23 Like a coating of silver dross on earthenware are fervent [a] lips with an evil heart.

24 Enemies disguise themselves with their lips, but in their hearts they harbor deceit.

25 Though their speech is charming, do not believe them, for seven abominations fill their hearts.

26 Their malice may be concealed by deception, but their wickedness will be exposed in the assembly.

27 Whoever digs a pit will fall into it; if someone rolls a stone, it will roll back on them.

28 A lying tongue hates those it hurts, and a flattering mouth works ruin.

Proverbs 26 - Prayer

Father, help me remain humble and not have too high an opinion of myself. Help me not walk my own path. Keep me close to You and allow me to hear Your voice clearly so I can avoid foolish ways.

I ask that You search my heart and my life and show me if there is any foolish way in me. Show me where I need to repent and change, so I can avoid living like a fool in any area of my life.

What do You say about a fool?

- Proverbs 1:5-7 - Despises wisdom and instruction
- Proverbs 1:22 - Hates knowledge
- Proverbs 10:18-19 - Slanders
- Proverbs 10:21 - No work ethic
- Proverbs 12:15 - Does not listen but is arrogant
- Proverbs 12:22-23 - Spews ignorance to others
- Proverbs 14:8 - Deceives others
- Proverbs 14:9 - Makes fun of humility and righteousness
- Proverbs 15:2 - Speaks foolish things
- Proverbs 15:14 - Echo chamber of ignorance
- Proverbs 18:2-3 - Speaks first and disdains to hear
- Proverbs 18:13 - Quick to speak and slow to hear
- Proverbs 23:9 - Despises the truth
- Proverbs 29:20 - Loves to talk

Empower me, Lord, to do whatever work I have to do today with diligence and excellence. Help me avoid procrastinating and slothfulness. I want to be a good example to those I work around, and a good witness for You.

Allow me not to be a contentious person or given to gossip or deceit in any way. Help me deal honestly with others and with integrity.

Keep my lips from speaking lies or flattery, and allow me to speak the truth in love in all my dealings with people today.

What I'm hearing God say today:

PROVERBS 27

1 Do not boast about tomorrow, for you do not know what a day may bring.

2 Let someone else praise you, and not your own mouth; an outsider, and not your own lips.

3 Stone is heavy and sand a burden, but a fool's provocation is heavier than both.

4 Anger is cruel and fury overwhelming, but who can stand before jealousy?

5 Better is open rebuke than hidden love.

6 Wounds from a friend can be trusted, but an enemy multiplies kisses.

7 One who is full loathes honey from the comb, but to the hungry even what is bitter tastes sweet.

8 Like a bird that flees its nest is anyone who flees from home.

9 Perfume and incense bring joy to the heart, and the pleasantness of a friend springs from their heartfelt advice.

10 Do not forsake your friend or a friend of your family, and do not go to your relative's house when disaster strikes you– better a neighbor nearby than a relative far away.

11 Be wise, my son, and bring joy to my heart; then I can answer anyone who treats me with contempt.

12 The prudent see danger and take refuge, but the simple keep going and pay the penalty.

13 Take the garment of one who puts up security for a stranger; hold it in pledge if it is done for an outsider.

14 If anyone loudly blesses their neighbor early in the morning, it will be taken as a curse.

15 A quarrelsome wife is like the dripping of a leaky roof in a rainstorm;

16 restraining her is like restraining the wind or grasping oil with the hand.

17 As iron sharpens iron, so one person sharpens another.

18 The one who guards a fig tree will eat its fruit, and whoever protects their master will be honored.

19 As water reflects the face, so one's life reflects the heart.

20 Death and Destruction are never satisfied, and neither are human eyes.

21 The crucible for silver and the furnace for gold, but people are tested by their praise.

22 Though you grind a fool in a mortar, grinding them like grain with a pestle, you will not remove their folly from them.

23 Be sure you know the condition of your flocks, give careful attention to your herds;

24 for riches do not endure forever, and a crown is not secure for all generations.

25 When the hay is removed and new growth appears and the grass from the hills is gathered in,

26 the lambs will provide you with clothing, and the goats with the price of a field.

27 You will have plenty of goats' milk to feed your family and to nourish your female servants.

Proverbs 27 - Prayer

Thank You, Father that You alone know what is in store for me today. I submit my day - my plans, my to-do list and all of my interactions with others to You and ask for Your wisdom, discernment and protection.

I ask that You grant me a heart of humility, diligence, and integrity - knowing that every good gift comes from Your hand and without You I can accomplish nothing of significance today. Without You living and working in and through me, I am only living for myself and my glory.

Father, I am truly thankful for the love, counsel, and prayers of my close friends today. Bless them please for their loyal love and faithful friendship.

Again today, Lord, I ask that I may do my work unto You and for Your glory. Help me to bring prosperity to my boss and my employer, and even to my fellow employees.

(As a boss/employer myself - I ask that You grant me grace to treat my employees with respect and fairness and to represent You well in all my dealings with them.)

Search my heart, Lord, and cleanse me from sin and anything in my heart/life that is not pleasing to You. Keep me from pondering Satan's lies, deceptions, and accusations - and to reject them by the truth and power of Your Word. Help me resist him and give him no ground in my life.

Allow me to be a good steward of all You have entrusted to my care. Everything I am, and everything I have is from You. Keep me thankful for all the blessings You have lavished upon me, and humbled by Your great love for me.

Thank You that You promise to provide all of my needs through Your riches in Christ Jesus.

What I'm hearing God say today:

PROVERBS 28

1 The wicked flee though no one pursues, but the righteous are as bold as a lion.

2 When a country is rebellious, it has many rulers, but a ruler with discernment and knowledge maintains order.

3 A ruler [a] who oppresses the poor is like a driving rain that leaves no crops.

4 Those who forsake instruction praise the wicked, but those who heed it resist them.

5 Evildoers do not understand what is right, but those who seek the LORD understand it fully.

6 Better the poor whose walk is blameless than the rich whose ways are perverse.

7 A discerning son heeds instruction, but a companion of gluttons disgraces his father.

8 Whoever increases wealth by taking interest or profit from the poor amasses it for another, who will be kind to the poor.

9 If anyone turns a deaf ear to my instruction, even their prayers are detestable.

10 Whoever leads the upright along an evil path will fall into their own trap, but the blameless will receive a good inheritance.

11 The rich are wise in their own eyes; one who is poor and discerning sees how deluded they are.

12 When the righteous triumph, there is great elation; but when the wicked rise to power, people go into hiding.

13 Whoever conceals their sins does not prosper, but the one who confesses and renounces them finds mercy.

14 Blessed is the one who always trembles before God, but whoever hardens their heart falls into trouble.

15 Like a roaring lion or a charging bear is a wicked ruler over a helpless people.

16 A tyrannical ruler practices extortion, but one who hates ill-gotten gain will enjoy a long reign.

17 Anyone tormented by the guilt of murder will seek refuge in the grave; let no one hold them back.

18 The one whose walk is blameless is kept safe, but the one whose ways are perverse will fall into the pit. [b]

19 Those who work their land will have abundant food, but those who chase fantasies will have their fill of poverty.

20 A faithful person will be richly blessed, but one eager to get rich will not go unpunished.

21 To show partiality is not good– yet a person will do wrong for a piece of bread.

22 The stingy are eager to get rich and are unaware that poverty awaits them.

23 Whoever rebukes a person will in the end gain favor rather than one who has a flattering tongue.

24 Whoever robs their father or mother and says, "It's not wrong," is partner to one who destroys.

25 The greedy stir up conflict, but those who trust in the LORD will prosper.

26 Those who trust in themselves are fools, but those who walk in wisdom are kept safe.

27 Those who give to the poor will lack nothing, but those who close their eyes to them receive many curses.

28 When the wicked rise to power, people go into hiding; but when the wicked perish, the righteous thrive.

Proverbs 28 - Prayer

Thank You, Lord that I can face today with confidence and hope knowing I am Your child. Thank You for the blood of Jesus that cleanses me and Your Spirit Who empowers me. My righteousness is found in You, and I can face my future with confidence.

I rejoice today as I walk with You, and trust Your sovereign leadership in my life.

Search my heart, Lord and show me any sin I need to confess and any evil way in me. I repent today of _____
_____
_____
_____

and any thought, word, or deed that would keep me from experiencing the joy of Your presence. I forsake these sins and thank You that You are faithful and just to forgive me and cleanse me.

Father, would you give me a heart that longs to know You and Your Word? I want to know You and not just know about You. I want to hide Your Word in my heart that I might not sin against You, and that I will be equipped to battle the enemy effectively.

Allow me once again to work diligently today and do my work as unto You. Help me to be faithful in every task You entrust to me, and to trust You with my financial resources.

Grant me a thankful, generous heart - free from greed and the love of money. May I be generous to the poor and a wise steward of the resources You provide.

I trust You today, Father, and bring my heart, mind, and will under Your sovereignty authority.

I bring the authority, rule, and dominion of the Lord Jesus Christ and the full work of Christ over my life today: over my marriage, my home, my children and grandchildren, my work, my finances and over all my earthly domain.

What I'm hearing God say today:

PROVERBS 29

1 Whoever remains stiff-necked after many rebukes will suddenly be destroyed—without remedy.

2 When the righteous thrive, the people rejoice; when the wicked rule, the people groan.

3 A man who loves wisdom brings joy to his father, but a companion of prostitutes squanders his wealth.

4 By justice a king gives a country stability, but those who are greedy for [a] bribes tear it down.

5 Those who flatter their neighbors are spreading nets for their feet.

6 Evildoers are snared by their own sin, but the righteous shout for joy and are glad.

7 The righteous care about justice for the poor, but the wicked have no such concern.

8 Mockers stir up a city, but the wise turn away anger.

9 If a wise person goes to court with a fool, the fool rages and scoffs, and there is no peace.

10 The bloodthirsty hate a person of integrity and seek to kill the upright.

11 Fools give full vent to their rage, but the wise bring calm in the end.

12 If a ruler listens to lies, all his officials become wicked.

13 The poor and the oppressor have this in common: The LORD gives sight to the eyes of both.

14 If a king judges the poor with fairness, his throne will be established forever.

15 A rod and a reprimand impart wisdom, but a child left undisciplined disgraces its mother.

16 When the wicked thrive, so does sin, but the righteous will see their downfall.

17 Discipline your children, and they will give you peace; they will bring you the delights you desire.

18 Where there is no revelation, people cast off restraint; but blessed is the one who heeds wisdom's instruction.

19 Servants cannot be corrected by mere words; though they understand, they will not respond.

20 Do you see someone who speaks in haste? There is more hope for a fool than for them.

21 A servant pampered from youth will turn out to be insolent.

22 An angry person stirs up conflict, and a hot-tempered person commits many sins.

23 Pride brings a person low, but the lowly in spirit gain honor.

24 The accomplices of thieves are their own enemies; they are put under oath and dare not testify.

25 Fear of man will prove to be a snare, but whoever trusts in the LORD is kept safe.

26 Many seek an audience with a ruler, but it is from the LORD that one gets justice.

27 The righteous detest the dishonest; the wicked detest the upright.

Proverbs 29 - Prayer

Father, grant me a heart that loves wisdom and is eager to know Your Word. Help me to quickly respond to any conviction and correction by Your Spirit.

Help me to live righteously today and avoid the schemes and snares of the enemy.

I rejoice today to be Your child and am forever grateful that You chose me. My name is forever written in Your Book of Life and I am a joint heir with Jesus of a glorious, eternal inheritance.

I sing and rejoice that Your plans for me only bring good things in my life - even if they may not seem good at the time.

You again remind me today to discipline wisely the children under my care. In doing so, You assure me they will not bring us shame, but rather happiness. Give me courage to love and lead in this area and to avoid passivity in this critical area of my family.

Help me to not be hasty with my words today but to listen well and ponder my words before I speak. Grant me the fruit of self-control today, and allow me to be quick to hear and slow to speak in order to avoid anger and respond with grace and truth. Keep me from a prideful heart, Lord and help me to walk in humility today as I remember that everything I have is from You and without You I can do nothing.

Allow me to not fear people and what they may think or say - but rather to fear You and care more about pleasing You than people.

I place my trust in You, Father, and ask that You guide my thoughts and my actions as I seek to live a life of integrity and righteousness.

What I'm hearing God say today:

PROVERBS 30

1 The sayings of Agur son of Jakeh—an inspired utterance. This man's utterance to Ithiel: "I am weary, God, but I can prevail.

2 Surely I am only a brute, not a man; I do not have human understanding.

3 I have not learned wisdom, nor have I attained to the knowledge of the Holy One.

4 Who has gone up to heaven and come down? Whose hands have gathered up the wind? Who has wrapped up the waters in a cloak? Who has established all the ends of the earth? What is his name, and what is the name of his son? Surely you know!

5 Every word of God is flawless; he is a shield to those who take refuge in him.

6 Do not add to his words, or he will rebuke you and prove you a liar.

7 "Two things I ask of you, LORD ; do not refuse me before I die:

8 Keep falsehood and lies far from me; give me neither poverty nor riches, but give me only my daily bread.

9 Otherwise, I may have too much and disown you and say, 'Who is the LORD ?' Or I may become poor and steal, and so dishonor the name of my God.

10 "Do not slander a servant to their master, or they will curse you, and you will pay for it.

11 "There are those who curse their fathers and do not bless their mothers;

12 those who are pure in their own eyes and yet are not cleansed of their filth;

13 those whose eyes are ever so haughty, whose glances are so disdainful;

14 those whose teeth are swords and whose jaws are set with knives to devour the poor from the earth and the needy from among mankind.

15 "The leech has two daughters. 'Give! Give!' they cry. "There are three things that are never satisfied, four that never say, 'Enough!':

16 the grave, the barren womb, land, which is never satisfied with water, and fire, which never says, 'Enough!'

17 "The eye that mocks a father, that scorns an aged mother, will be pecked out by the ravens of the valley, will be eaten by the vultures.

18 "There are three things that are too amazing for me, four that I do not understand:

19 the way of an eagle in the sky, the way of a snake on a rock, the way of a ship on the high seas, and the way of a man with a young woman.

20 "This is the way of an adulterous woman: She eats and wipes her mouth and says, 'I've done nothing wrong.'

21 "Under three things the earth trembles, under four it cannot bear up:

22 a servant who becomes king, a godless fool who gets plenty to eat,

23 a contemptible woman who gets married, and a servant who displaces her mistress.

24 "Four things on earth are small, yet they are extremely wise:

25 Ants are creatures of little strength, yet they store up their food in the summer;

26 hyraxes are creatures of little power, yet they make their home in the crags;

27 locusts have no king, yet they advance together in ranks;

28 a lizard can be caught with the hand, yet it is found in kings' palaces.

29 "There are three things that are stately in their stride, four that move with stately bearing:

30 a lion, mighty among beasts, who retreats before nothing;

31 a strutting rooster, a he-goat, and a king secure against revolt.

32 "If you play the fool and exalt yourself, or if you plan evil, clap your hand over your mouth!

33 For as churning cream produces butter, and as twisting the nose produces blood, so stirring up anger produces strife.

Proverbs 30 - Prayer

Father, thank You that You are a shield and a refuge for me today. When I am weary from battle, and heavy laden from life - I can come to You for rest and restoration.

Help me to stay alert to evil and to the lion's roar. My adversary does not sleep, so I need to stay equally vigilant if I am to live in victory.

Allow me to walk in Your truth and to reject falsehood of any kind that tempts me to think or speak what is untrue. Satan is a liar and the father of all lies. I do not want to give him any ground or authority in my life by joining him in lies.

Help me to quickly recognize his lies and to be able to speak Your truth in response.

Thank You for the financial resources You provide for me. Help me to work hard, but also to learn to be content whether I have plenty or little.

I know You will supply all my needs through Your riches in Christ, and I have no reason to envy or be jealous of others.

Nature reminds me, Lord, of Your creativity and majesty, and I can learn truth by observing the wonder of Your creation.

Would You keep me from acting foolishly or planning evil in any way? Help guard my heart from anger and allow me to walk in love and grace toward others today.

What I'm hearing God say today:

PROVERBS 31

1 The sayings of King Lemuel—an inspired utterance his mother taught him.

2 Listen, my son! Listen, son of my womb! Listen, my son, the answer to my prayers!

3 Do not spend your strength [a] on women, your vigor on those who ruin kings.

4 It is not for kings, Lemuel— it is not for kings to drink wine, not for rulers to crave beer,

5 lest they drink and forget what has been decreed, and deprive all the oppressed of their rights.

6 Let beer be for those who are perishing, wine for those who are in anguish!

7 Let them drink and forget their poverty and remember their misery no more.

8 Speak up for those who cannot speak for themselves, for the rights of all who are destitute.

9 Speak up and judge fairly; defend the rights of the poor and needy.

Epilogue: The Wife of Noble Character

10 A wife of noble character who can find? She is worth far more than rubies.

11 Her husband has full confidence in her and lacks nothing of value.

12 She brings him good, not harm, all the days of her life.

13 She selects wool and flax and works with eager hands.

14 She is like the merchant ships, bringing her food from afar.

15 She gets up while it is still night; she provides food for her family and portions for her female servants.

16 She considers a field and buys it; out of her earnings she plants a vineyard.

17 She sets about her work vigorously; her arms are strong for her tasks.

18 She sees that her trading is profitable, and her lamp does not go out at night.

19 In her hand she holds the distaff and grasps the spindle with her fingers.

20 She opens her arms to the poor and extends her hands to the needy.

21 When it snows, she has no fear for her household; for all of them are clothed in scarlet.

22 She makes coverings for her bed; she is clothed in fine linen and purple.

23 Her husband is respected at the city gate, where he takes his seat among the elders of the land.

24 She makes linen garments and sells them, and supplies the merchants with sashes.

25 She is clothed with strength and dignity; she can laugh at the days to come.

26 She speaks with wisdom, and faithful instruction is on her tongue.

27 She watches over the affairs of her household and does not eat the bread of idleness.

28 Her children arise and call her blessed; her husband also, and he praises her:

29 "Many women do noble things, but you surpass them all."

30 Charm is deceptive, and beauty is fleeting; but a woman who fears the LORD is to be praised.

31 Honor her for all that her hands have done, and let her works bring her praise at the city gate.

Proverbs 31 - Prayer

Father, grant me strength today to walk in Your ways and embrace all that You have for me.

Keep me from fruitless and dangerous paths, and guide me into all truth I pray. Your Word says You will guide me in paths of righteousness, so I claim that truth over me today.

Help me to judge rightly and to be generous to those around me who are less fortunate.

Married: Father, I thank You for my wife. I ask that You continue to work in her heart to develop noble, Godly character. Give her a heart to desire You first in all things and to please You in all her ways.

Help me, Lord, to show her honor and to put her needs ahead of my own. I need Your grace to love and forgive "as" You have loved and forgiven me.

Father, thank You for the gifts, skills and abilities You have given my wife. I ask that You allow her ample opportunity to grow and flourish in those gifts and help me to encourage her to do so.

I acknowledge that my wife is a gift from You and Your beloved daughter. Remind me daily of that truth and allow me to love her accordingly, and to appreciate such a wonderful, personal gift from You.

Help me not only heed Your admonition to "credit her' and "praise her" personally, but also in front of our children, our friends, our parents and others frequently. I want her to know how very proud I am of her and that she is doing a wonderful job - remembering that love is a verb, and my actions need to reflect my thoughts.

Father, you call me to love my wife "as" You love me - which speaks of loving her unconditionally, and laying my life down for her. I am desperate for You to empower me to love her that way, and to never think I can place any conditions on obeying Your command.

What I'm hearing God say today:

www.ingramcontent.com/pod-product-compliance
Lightning Source LLC
Chambersburg PA
CBHW081456040426
42446CB00016B/3268